Michigan's Town and Country Inns

Michigan's Town & Country INNS

Third Edition

Susan Newhof Pyle and Stephen J. Pyle

The University of Michigan Press

Ann Arbor

Library of Congress Cataloging-in-Publication Data

Pyle, Susan Newhof, 1952–
   Michigan's town & country inns.

   Includes index.
   1. Hotels, taverns, etc.—Michigan—Directories.
2. Bed and breakfast accommodations—Michigan—
Directories.   I. Pyle, Stephen J., 1950–   .   II. Title.
III. Title: Michigan's town and country inns.
TX907.P95   1989   647'.9477401   86-30877
ISBN 0-472-08087-3 (pbk.)

*To Carole Eberly
and Russell McKee*

Acknowledgments

This book that you hold in your hands is evidence that dreams do come true. Many individuals, over the past decade, helped us put the right pieces together to make this project work, and we offer sincere thanks to the following: to Mary Erwin, University of Michigan Press acquisitions editor, who gave us the greatest thrill of our life when she said, "Better start writing, the Board approved your manuscript," and who has guided us every step of the way; to Jim Purvis for first-edition manuscript editing and for helping Susan understand why punctuation isn't optional; to David Wright (gift of the gods) for third-edition editing and for nuturing our academic endeavors; to Nada P. Davis, trusted assistant, for wit, perspective, and for making possible the time away from work to complete research; to Kirby Milton and Steve Beck for teaching photographic excellence by word and example; to friends who have fostered our progress and remained close in spite of research weekends and deadlines that often made us unavailable, unresponsive, and preoccupied; and to all the innkeepers who have befriended, advised, encouraged, and promoted us. A large portion of the success of this book belongs to all of you.

Contents

Introduction

There was a time in this state when roadhouses and small hotels were scattered all along the major routes between cities. They ranged from steamy taverns with primitive sleeping quarters upstairs or "around the back" to elegant inns with fine food and furnishings. Many of the lodgings went out of business and were abandoned when freeways came along, routing travelers around small towns and off the back roads. Some were converted to restaurants or office buildings, some caught fire. Some just quietly crumbled until they were finally torn down.

A few of the grand old places have survived the decades of transition and are well known because of their prominent roles in history and their undisputed charm. But with a growing interest in preserving our historic architecture and a yearning in travelers for lodging that is personalized, warm, and memorable, more than 200 inns and bed-and-breakfast homes have opened or reopened throughout Michigan in less than half a decade.

With this third edition, we take you on another adventure across Michigan's two peninsulas and into more than 70 such accommodations. Some are like tiny museums full of turn-of-the-century treasures. Some are rugged and rustic and will intoxicate you with the smell of wood and fresh air and breakfast cooking. They are as different from each other as the individuals who run them and their differences are, in part, what makes them so endearing.

The inns and bed-and-breakfast homes we selected for this edition fit complex, but not rigid, criteria. When deciding which to include, we looked for the following:

- excellence in hospitality
- the presence of an innkeeper or manager who sees to it that guests are well cared for
- cleanliness
- three or more guest rooms (you will find some exceptions)
- attractive and appropriate furnishings placed with the guest in mind
- good food included with the room or available on the premises
- support for other innkeepers and the bed-and-breakfast industry
- a lodging fully open for at least one year

Finally, and perhaps most importantly, we looked for the warmth and enthusiasm that put guests at ease as soon as they walk in the door and for the personal touches that make their visit memorable.

We have tried to portray each place accurately and do not expect that you will like all of them—indeed, if you did, it might mean they were losing the distinctiveness that makes some of them so fiercely appealing. To help you choose the accommodations that will best suit you, please consider the following information before you make reservations.

- First, a little about innkeepers because they are the heart and soul of most inns. It is often in their living room that you will spend the evening chatting with other guests and in their kitchen or dining room that you will continue the conversations over morning coffee. An innkeeper gives a place its flavor and sets the mood, and for that reason you will find an emphasis placed on them in many of the descriptions. We want you to know a little about them so you will have a better feel for the places you visit.

Some innkeepers, you will find, are accomplished artists, athletes, or scholars. A few have had distinguished military careers. Some are quiet and pensive, others are flamboyant. Generally, the smaller the inn, the greater the presence of the innkeeper. Almost without exception, we discovered that innkeepers take great pride in being able to sense which guests would like to be alone and which are up for group discussions on the front porch that may go on until dawn.

Innkeepers have told us that many of their guests make their own beds, send thank-you letters, bring gifts on subsequent visits, and have become warm friends. They say their lives are enriched by their guests. Guests have said they visited an inn the first time because of the furnishings and location; they returned because of the innkeepers.

- Many inns and bed-and-breakfast homes do not feature a private bathroom with each sleeping room. If shared or down-the-hall bathrooms do not appeal to you, ask the innkeeper about rest room arrangements. For example, will it make a difference to you if you share a bathroom with one other room? with two? with six?

- The beds at inns vary greatly. Some offer only twin beds; others feature king- or queen-sized, or custom-made antique treasures. Remember that most turn-of-the-century people were shorter than we are today—and so were their beds. If it matters to you, ask about bed sizes.

• Some people can fall asleep on anything. Some require firm, lump-less mattresses. If you fall into the latter category, ask if the mattresses are new or original equipment.

• If it applies, inquire about the inn's policy regarding smoking and pets. And while we are on the subject . . .

• In this edition, we have added a new component to Vitals: pets in residence. It lists primarily dogs and cats that live on the premises or that guests may come in contact with. In most cases, we have found innkeeper's pets to be well-behaved and their owners willing to keep them tucked out of sight at a guest's request. If you are bothered by the presence of a pet, take the innkeeper aside and mention it. They may not be aware of the offense. If you have allergies, phobias, or pet peeves, ask the innkeepers if they keep pets in the house and, further, if the animals are ever allowed into quarters that are shared by guests.

• If you are planning to travel with children, be sure to mention them when you call for a reservation.

• Some inns have lockless sleeping room doors. Will that bother you?

• Ask what will be included in your room rate: meals, cleaning ser-vice, taxi or shuttle service, afternoon tea, admission to local points of interest, access to recreation areas and equipment (tennis courts, bicy-cles, sailboats, skis, etc.), tips, parking? In this book we have primarily provided information on food or meals included in the price of the room.

• Some of the older inns have built new additions onto the original structure or have constructed separate accommodations elsewhere on the grounds. If you have a preference as to wing, section, floor, or building, let the innkeeper know before you make the reservation and emphasize no substitutions.

• Many inns have a wide range of room prices because of the variety in rooms. If you are quoted a room rate that is more than what you want to spend, ask if a less expensive room is available. If the time of your visit is not important, consider traveling in the off-season. A great many of the inns discount rates substantially after fall colors and before Me-morial Day. Many also have special business rates, discounts for ex-tended stays, and discounts for groups renting all the rooms. Rates are listed in this book to give you an idea of the range available. Most are peak-season prices. They are updated as close to press time as possible but may be slightly different from those quoted to you at the time you make reservations. They are subject to change without notice.

• Many inns and bed and breakfast homes are not set up to process credit card payments. If you plan to pay for your room with anything other than cash, when you make a reservation, ask for the house policy on payment methods.

• And now, two words about making reservations. Do. Always. Remember that many of the places described here are private homes. Most do not have all-night desk clerks. They want to know when you are coming, and they do not want to find you unannounced on their doorstep at 11:00 P.M. With advance notice, you will find innkeepers to be some of friendliest people you will ever meet.

We have spent at least a few hours at each lodging covered here, and in most cases we stayed overnight. During the past six years of researching, many innkeepers have extended to us house courtesies, which have been accepted when logistically possible. We are grateful to the innkeepers for their gracious hospitality. They enabled us to log the several thousand miles of travel it took to compile this firsthand information.

In every case, they have opened all doors to our inspection and have been candid about the offerings and limitations of their accommodations. Nobody likes to see a guest unhappy with a misrepresented inn . . . least of all the innkeeper. With that said, it should be noted that innkeepers paid no fees to be included in this book.

We've joked about starting a respite care service for innkeepers. Their hours are long, and during busy seasons their breaks are few. We share a deep respect for them and for their pioneering spirit in this growing Michigan industry. Their concern for your comfort and their dedication to preserving a part of this state's history enriches us all.

Now, to you, dear reader. What do you think about all this? Have you stayed at inns and bed-and-breakfast homes yet? Are you a seasoned traveler? Do you have favorites and have we included them? Have you discovered a wonderful new, out-of-the-way place that we should know about? Write to us in care of our publisher: University of Michigan Press, P.O. Box 1104 MTCI, Ann Arbor, MI 48106. We look forward to hearing from you.

The Inns

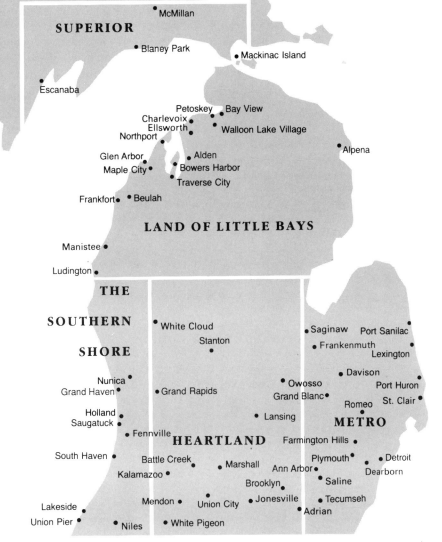

Big Bay

SUPERIOR

McMillan

Blaney Park

Mackinac Island

Escanaba

Petoskey   Bay View
Charlevoix
Ellsworth   Walloon Lake Village
Northport

Alpena

Glen Arbor   Alden
Maple City   Bowers Harbor
Traverse City

Frankfort   Beulah

LAND OF LITTLE BAYS

Manistee

Ludington

THE

SOUTHERN

SHORE

White Cloud   Saginaw   Port Sanilac
Stanton   Frankenmuth
                                          Lexington

                                     Davison
Nunica   Owosso   Port Huron
Grand Haven   Grand Rapids   Grand Blanc   St. Clair
                                          Romeo
Holland   Lansing
Saugatuck   METRO

Fennville   HEARTLAND   Farmington Hills
South Haven   Plymouth   Detroit
          Battle Creek   Dearborn
Kalamazoo   Marshall   Ann Arbor
                        Brooklyn   Saline
Lakeside   Mendon   Union City   Jonesville   Tecumseh
Union Pier   Adrian
      Niles   White Pigeon

**Big Bay Point Lighthouse Bed
    and Breakfast,** *Big Bay*
Celibeth House, *Blaney Park*
Helmer House Inn, *McMillan*
House of Ludington, *Escanaba*
Metivier Inn, *Mackinac Island*

Superior

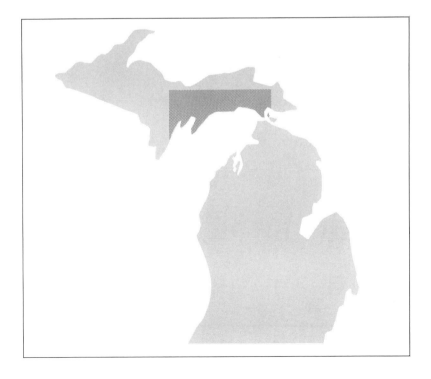

Big Bay Point Lighthouse Bed and Breakfast
Big Bay

Twenty-six miles north of Marquette on the Lake Superior shore is a quiet little town called Big Bay. It is a bit famous—it was the setting for the movie "Anatomy of a Murder" written by Upper Peninsula author Judge John Voelker, alias Robert Traver. The locals, according to a resident tour guide, are very concerned about the quality of life. That, says Buck Gotschall with a chuckle, means not working more than twenty hours per week.

Buck is owner and keeper of the Big Bay Point Lighthouse, a rock-solid structure built in 1896 four miles northeast of town on a granite bluff at the edge of Lake Superior. He has lived and worked in these

parts for years; in fact, he sold recreational wilderness real estate for a while and managed an office on the Yellow Dog River that had no electricity. He bought the lighthouse in December, 1986, and had his first bed-and-breakfast guests the following January. Since then, hundreds of visitors have come to this remote corner of the state to embrace the slow pace and explore the wild backcountry that stretches for miles around Big Bay.

The lighthouse has a nearly mirror-image floor plan originally designed to accommodate the lighthouse keeper and his family in one half, the assistant and his family in the other. Buck offers six of the sleeping rooms for bed-and-breakfast guests. They are of varying sizes and all have views of the lake or the surrounding woods and grounds. The furnishings are appropriately casual for this rugged outpost, yet they are attractive and comfortable. The spacious first-floor living room and dining room have several interior brick walls that provide a handsome backdrop for yellow pine woodwork, nautical items, books on sailing and the out-of-doors, and lighthouse art work.

Several years ago, the Coast Guard decommissioned the beacon in the old lighthouse tower and replaced it with an innocuous but equally effective pole lamp in the side yard. The tower is still open, however, and you are welcome to climb the winding stairs to the top where you

will be treated to a view of the vast lake and its rocky shoreline, and of the Huron Mountains that rise to the east. If you visit in early summer, when the sun does not set until well after 10:00 P.M., you may see vivid displays of rose, yellow, and sapphire in the sky that rise and melt into the lake before the stars finally come out. Buck says the aurora borealis is also breathtaking.

Outdoor enthusiasts will find plenty to do here. For starters, the lighthouse sits on five acres of lawn adjacent to fifty-three acres of forest and is bordered by 4,500 feet of Lake Superior shoreline. Buck will arrange side trips for you if you want to explore the area. He has an arsenal of guides—all locals—whose services, to name a few, include hikes to waterfalls, a visit to a logging camp, photography field trips, skiing, kayaking, mountain biking, and history lessons. Rates range from $50 to $100 a day for up to eight persons.

Buck is a busy guy with a score of hobbies and a colorful past. He keeps an organic garden, thrives on physical activity, and is a former tennis pro. During the summer, he is frequently off the lighthouse grounds from early afternoon until early evening. Such was the case when we arrived. A note detailing all the information we needed to make ourselves at home was taped to the door, along with two "Keeper's Helper" buttons.

Whatever his daily schedule might be, Buck sets aside the morning to be with his guests. He joined us over breakfast, which included a mouth-watering smoothie made with yogurt and fresh fruit and a flavorful, homemade, stick-to-the-ribs bread.

"I sell peace and quiet," says Buck. "And the coffeepot is always on."

Vitals

rooms: 6, 4 with private bath, 2 share 1 bath

pets: no

pets in residence: none

smoking: no

open season: year-round

rates: $75 through $125 double occupancy, discounts for second night

rates include: breakfast

owner/innkeeper:
Buck Gotschall
#3 Lighthouse Road
Big Bay, MI 49808
(906) 345-9957

Celibeth House
Blaney Park

In 1985, the entire town of Blaney Park went up on the auction block. Now, it was not much of a town, but it did have a couple big lodges, a few houses and storefronts, some small cabins, and one mansion at the top of a hill to the north. Elsa Strom had her eye on the mansion, and the day after the auction, she inquired about it, only to find that it had not sold. She made an offer and by the end of the summer, it was hers.

Elsa had grown up not far from Blaney Park. Her father and mother settled in Corinne in 1909, enticed by the promises of the logging industry. When logging gave out, her father became Corinne's postmaster. Elsa remembers when Blaney Park was a thriving resort town built by the Wisconsin Land and Lumber Company. People came from all over the Midwest to enjoy the clean Upper Peninsula air, golf, tennis, swimming, and bountiful meals served three times daily at a big pine lodge. Blaney Park closed in 1970. Although there were a few efforts to resurrect the resort, all failed, leaving the owner to auction it piece by piece.

Elsa's beautiful home was built in 1895 as a private residence for the Mueller family. The Earles, who owned the Wisconsin Land and Lumber Company, acquired it in 1911 and called it Celibeth—a combination of the names of two cousins Cecilia and Elizabeth. By the time Elsa got it, the home was in need of repair and redecorating, but it was still sound. She went to work first on the east-facing sun porch that became the breakfast room. It is a cheery sight first thing in the morning with its white walls and furnishings, vases of fresh flowers from Elsa's gardens, and sunlight filtering through tall cedars. Delicate paper window blinds sport a whimsical tulip design. The eight sleeping rooms are large and tastefully decorated with art, antiques, heirlooms, and treasures that Elsa had been collecting for years. In several rooms, you will find an original wainscotting treatment called Coraflek that Elsa was able to preserve. Others have been newly papered with pretty floral prints. Each room has a private bath.

In late summer, Elsa wrote to say that she added a twelve-by-thirty-foot deck off the breakfast room, and guests enjoyed watching dozens of hummingbirds dart about.

This is a comfortable home where you can settle in for a few days and absorb the stillness of the country. Ask Elsa about the nature trails she has been building on Celibeth's eighty-five acres. They reach north to Lake Anne Louise where you will find cranes, loons, bluebirds, and good fishing. If you are looking for activities, you will enjoy Celibeth's central location. It is less than an hour's drive to Seney National Refuge, Tahquamenon Falls, Grand Marais and Pictured Rocks, the ghost town of Fayette, and the beaches at Lake Michigan or Lake Superior.

Vitals

rooms: 8 with private baths

pets: no

pets in residence: 2 cats, not permitted in sleeping rooms

smoking: discouraged inside, but OK on the enclosed front porch

open season: May 1 through December 1

rates: $35 double occupancy, rooms with sleeping alcove or 2 double beds are $45

rates include: breakfast

owner/innkeeper:
Elsa Strom
Blaney Park Road, M-77
Route 1, Box 58A
Blaney Park, MI 49836
(906) 283-3409

Helmer House Inn
McMillan

More than one hundred years ago, the Reverend Mills, a Presbyterian minister, came to the shores of Big Manistique Lake and built a mission house to help accommodate early settlers. In 1887, Gale Helmer purchased the mission and converted it into a successful lakeside resort and general store. The area became a center of activity. It was a convenient halfway point between Curtis and McMillan, and the stagecoach and mail wagon stopped there.

When the federal government designated the site as a post office in 1904, they appointed Mr. Helmer postmaster and officially gave the four-corners his name. That same year, Charles and Jeanie Fyvie, who had earlier immigrated from Scotland, arrived in Helmer. They bought the resort and Charles took over as postmaster. The resort business thrived for several years.

As the 1950s were ushered in, the glorious days of clapboard resorts and dance pavilions were coming to an end, and the scene at

Helmer was changing drastically. The general store had closed. The old lodge and homestead were deteriorating and eventually abandoned.

Responsibility for the building fell to Rob Goldthorpe, grandson of the Fyvies, and one of three grandchildren to have been born at the old homestead. Faced with the choice of tearing down the building or fixing it, Rob and his wife Marge embarked on a complete renovation of the structure and reopened the Helmer House in 1982.

Like traditional old roadside inns, Helmer House has both a restaurant and sleeping quarters. The dining room seating is located where the wraparound porch once stretched along the front and south side of the house. The area is now enclosed and each table sits by a large window. Around the corner from the dining area is the living room where dinner patrons can wait for a table and overnight guests mingle among plush, overstuffed Victorian-era couches and family heirlooms.

The second- and third-floor sleeping rooms vary in size and are all furnished with lovely antiques. Fine old iron, brass, and wooden bedsteads come complete with thick feather comforters for cold U.P. nights.

Turn-of-the-century memorabilia decorate the rooms, and each has a dresser so you can unpack and stay for a while.

The Goldthorpes' daughter, Linda, is innkeeper now. She was raised in the Upper Peninsula and enjoys the sense of history that surrounds the family's inn. And she likes the weather.

"This is our favorite time of year," she exclaimed when we spoke in October and the snowbanks around the inn were already five inches high.

Helmer has a well-deserved reputation for good food. We enjoyed a superb whitefish dinner—it is all-you-can-eat—and were greeted the next morning with steaming French toast and fresh fruit. A full breakfast is served to all overnight guests. The dining room is open to the public Wednesday through Monday in the summer.

Vitals

rooms: 5 sleeping rooms that share a full bath on the second floor and a water closet on the third; 3 rooms have vanities with sinks

pets: no

pets in residence: none

smoking: yes in dining room, discouraged in sleeping rooms

open season: May through December

rates: $29 through $36 single, $34 through $45 double occupancy; $10 each additional person

rates include: full breakfast

owners: Robert and Marge Goldthorpe

innkeeper:

Linda Goldthorpe
County Road 417
McMillan, MI 49853
(906) 586-3204

House of Ludington
Escanaba

"I always liked this place," remembers Gerald Lancour, owner of the House of Ludington. And in the past century, so have thousands of others. The Atlantic City–style hotel at the foot of Ludington Street, on Little Bay de Noc, has courted travelers since 1868. Additions put on during the first few decades of its life brought the hotel's offerings to one hundred sleeping rooms and a livery stable for guests' horses.

Chicago businessman Pat Hayes bought the hotel in 1939. He was a flamboyant character and did much to perpetuate and enhance the House of Ludington's reputation for class and style. In 1959, he installed an exterior glass-walled elevator running up the front of the hotel, which gave guests an outstanding view of the bay as they ascended to their rooms. National and international personalities, stars, politicians, and figures from the underworld made the House of Ludington their home away from home.

In later years, as the economic climate and ownership changed, the

building grew old and business dropped. By the early 1980s, the hotel was vacant and deteriorating fast.

Gerald, his wife Vernice, and a sister-in-law and brother-in-law, were looking for a business to get into after retirement. They had planned to head for Florida until the forlorn old hotel caught Gerald's eye. Judging by its state of disrepair, he felt that he was looking at the last opportunity to save it, and he couldn't turn it down.

Their initial and most major renovation took three months and was masterful to say the least. The hotel is once again a proud landmark, a center of activity with the park and bay shore just across the street. And it is an enjoyable place to stay. All of the sleeping rooms have been individually redecorated in styles from contemporary to traditional. Some are furnished with original hotel pieces such as a matching bed and dresser with tiny, hand-painted, porcelain drawer pulls, each featuring a different scene. The rooms have private bathrooms and air-conditioning, and they are spotlessly clean and quiet. Many of the smaller rooms have been combined to make larger rooms and suites with

sitting areas, and guests still ride the famous glass elevator to get to their floor.

Meals are served with linen and fine table service in two elegant rooms on the main floor. The King George dining room has a very large, original fireplace with priceless silver and china from the hotel's early days displayed on its hearth and in beautiful old glass cases. Some of the original place settings are still used. The waiters are formally attired and they serve at a slow, easy pace so diners can relax and feel unrushed. Our orders of kastler ripchen and Wiener schnitzel were superb, and the whole dining experience remains a very pleasant memory.

Gerald and Vernice bought out their partners and now run the hotel side by side. Vernice's decorating talents and her eye for detail can be seen throughout the hotel, but an encapsulated sampling is her creation of a miniature Victorian home on display in the gift shop. The project took three years to complete and could hold your attention for hours. Take a look at it and see if you can figure out who ended up with the piece of cake missing from the pantry.

A high level of quality is apparent in every aspect of this historic hotel, as is warm hospitality from the people who work there.

Vitals

rooms: 25 with private baths

pets: up to discretion of innkeeper

pets in residence: none

smoking: yes

open season: year-round

rates: $54 through $58 double occupancy; $60 through $65 for small suites

rates include: room only

owners/innkeepers:
Gerald and Vernice Lancour
223 Ludington Street
Escanaba, MI 49829
(906) 786-4000

Metivier Inn
Mackinac Island

The Metivier Inn is located just one block back from the island's busy main street giving guests both easy access to the goings-on in this picturesque island village and quiet respite from it all.

This was the summer home of the Metivier family for decades before it caught the eye of Dr. Michael Bacon. Michael had summered on Mackinac Island as a child. After completing medical school with specialization in family practice from Michigan State University, he began providing relief coverage for the island doctor and eventually spent some time as the island clinic's primary physician. He was thrilled when he was able to purchase the estate from a member of the Metivier family several years ago, even though he was not sure what he would do with it.

In 1983, Michael and his wife, Jane, and her brother and sister-in-law, Ken and Diane Neyer, joined forces to convert the home to an inn. They skillfully added a third floor and the entire east wing, including a

distinctive turret. Then they extended the wide veranda the length of the inn so that it is impossible to tell where the old stops and the new begins.

Jane and Diane confidently took on the task of decorating the inn. They selected a country French theme and, against a backdrop of delicate French floral wall coverings, furnished the sleeping rooms with iron and brass, wicker, and four-poster beds; and pine accessories including handmade trunks and luggage stands. Antique wicker chairs and lounges are covered with crisp, cotton prints. From the smallest room to the largest suite with its sunny turret, they are all fresh, sophisticated, and pretty.

The first-floor lobby is furnished with a handsome Chippendale love seat, wing chairs, and pine dining tables. Breakfast is served buffet-style here and includes a choice of coffee cakes, croissants, juice, fruit, and beverages. When weather permits, guests can dine on the veranda amid white wicker tables and chairs and watch the island waking up.

Numerous old lilac trees surround the inn. We happened to arrive on the day of the island's lilac parade and found the whole town abloom, the lilacs' sweet scent filling the air. A walk around the inn to the backyard revealed a magnificent view of the Grand Hotel and its golf course, which borders the inn. We could also see the governor's mansion just up the hill.

It is an easy walk from the boat docks to Metivier. Bicycle-riding porters can assist you with luggage. Stables are just across the street. When you arrive at the inn, it is likely you will be greeted by managers Irma and Rodney Kujat, who have spent many summers on the island and are an excellent resource for information about the area.

Vitals

rooms: 15 with private baths, 2 are efficiencies

pets: no

pets in residence: none

smoking: discouraged

open season: early May to the middle of October

rates: $84 through $160 double occupancy, efficiencies $145 for up to 4 people

rates include: Continental breakfast

owners/innkeepers:
Jane and Michael Bacon, Diane and Ken Neyer

manager:
Irma and Rodney Kujat
Box 285
Mackinac Island, MI 49757
(906) 847-6234; winter: (616) 627-2055

Apple Beach Inn, *Northport*
Bay Bed and Breakfast, *Charlevoix*
Bed and Breakfast of Ludington, *Ludington*
Brookside Inn, *Beulah*
Chimney Corners, *Frankfort*
E. E. Douville Bed and Breakfast, *Manistee*
Fireside Inn, *Alpena*
The House on the Hill, *Ellsworth*
Leelanau Country Inn, *Maple City*
Neahtawanta Inn, *Traverse City (Bowers Harbor)*
North Shore Inn, *Northport*
The Old Mill Pond Inn, *Northport*
Plum Lane Inn, *Northport*
Stafford's Bay View Inn, *Petoskey*
The Sylvan Inn, *Glen Arbor*
The Terrace Inn, *Bay View*
Torch Lake Bed and Breakfast, *Alden*
Walloon Lake Inn, *Walloon Lake Village*
Warwickshire Inn, *Traverse City*
White Rose Country Inn, *Ludington*
Windermere Inn, *Beulah*

Land of Little Bays

Apple Beach Inn
Northport

Apple Beach Inn sits well back from the main road and is surrounded by mature maples, fruit trees, and patches of meadow. It was built as a private home in 1860 by a wealthy St. Louis family whose many interests included raising Morgan horses. "The family was quite fancy," the home's present owner, Mary Anne Taylor, told us. "I like to think about what I might have been wearing if I were here with them one hundred years ago, perhaps making my way up from the beach in a long dress and a bustle."

Mary Anne saw the home while on vacation in 1965 and was drawn to it immediately. She says simply, "I had to have it." It became the Taylors' summer home and might have remained so were it not for Mary Anne's mother, Bea Bowen, owner of the Plum Lane Inn just up the hill. Mary Anne began by taking some of Plum Lane's overflow or an occasional overbooking. She enjoyed it so much that she opened officially in early summer 1985. Like nearly all the innkeepers we have talked with, Mary Anne said the joy of owning a bed-and-breakfast home

is the guests. "They're like gifts," she explains. "They are the pivotal part of the whole experience."

Strong, clean lines and bright rooms characterize this fine old summer home. The living room has the front entry at one end and the back door at the other, a classic shotgun-style room—long and straight, and positioned to catch the lake breezes. The maple floor, white walls, and wicker and caned furniture enhance its cool, summery feeling. Off the living room, facing the lake, is a large, lovely sleeping room with a fireplace, private bath, and screen porch. Two smaller sleeping rooms on the second floor are papered with pretty print wallpaper and share a bath with a larger, dormitory-style room.

Breakfast is served in a sunny dining room. Our meal included a rich cheese quiche, hot cinnamon and walnut muffins, and a fresh fruit bowl garnished with mint that Mary Anne had picked near the beach that morning. On other days, the choices might include pancakes with maple syrup or a Pinconning cheese omelet. Soft classical music often plays in the background. Through the dining room's tall bay window you can look out onto a field of wildflowers and young trees, and beyond them to the blue waters of Traverse Bay.

The shore is edged with the old apple orchards that gave rise to the inn's name. A walking path will take you from the porch of the inn to the beach, where you will find a gazebo at the water's edge. It is very private and quiet—a delightful place to sip wine or lemonade in the late afternoon. Mary Anne joined us for coffee there in the morning and we watched the sun rise across the bay.

Even on cool, gray, rainy days, the lake and rolling surf have a mesmerizing quality that can hold our attention for hours. But should you find yourself at Apple Beach Inn on a dreary day and not so entranced by the lake, you will find ample good reading material and a fireplace to warm chilled bones. The town's shops and restaurants are within walking distance.

Vitals

rooms: 4, 1 with private bath; 3 that share 1 bath

pets: no

pets in residence: 1 cat, not allowed in guest rooms

smoking: on porch or outside only

open season: summer and fall

rates: $60 through $80 double occupancy

rates include: breakfast

owners/innkeepers:

Mary Anne and Herb Taylor
617 Shabwasung (M-22), Box 2
Northport, MI 49670
(616) 386-5022

Bay Bed and Breakfast
Charlevoix

On a warm summer afternoon in late July, we sipped iced tea with Marian Taylor-Beatty on the sixty-by-fourteen-foot deck of her bed-and-breakfast home overlooking Lake Michigan. The lake was very still, and Marian noted that it was a good day for floating on an inner tube. Marian knows the lake well. She and her husband Jack bought this home in the late 1960s while they were living in Mount Pleasant, and in the mid-1970s they moved in full-time. In 1984, they began offering lodging to bed and breakfast travelers.

The house sits atop a small bluff and is nestled in a woods of mature hemlock and hardwoods just fifty to sixty feet from the beach. Two sleeping rooms are available. The Tree Trunk Room on the first floor is furnished with a high wooden bedstead and is adjacent to the shared bathroom. The second floor Tree Top Room is reached by a spiral staircase from the living room. It has windows all around that give the room the feel of a private, well-decorated tree house. A large expanse of glass that reaches from the living room floor to its cathedral ceiling offers a spectacular view of the lake. There are scores of books to read and a cozy wood-burning stove for cold days.

Breakfast is ample and might include eggs Benedict Blackstone, which has the addition of a sautéed sliced tomato, or specialty pancakes with almonds. Smoked salmon from Marian's hometown of Newport, Oregon, is also often available.

The sandy shore beckons those who like to swim or beachcomb, and there is a lifetime supply of great skipping stones. Guests may also use Jack and Marian's canoe and inner tubes. Downhill and cross-country skiing are offered nearby for those looking for winter fun. The home is secluded and quiet, and just twelve miles from Charlevoix.

Vitals

rooms: 2 that share 1 bath

pets: no

pets in residence: 1 dog and 1 cat

smoking: outside only

open season: year-round

rates: $60 and $70 double occupancy

rates include: breakfast

owners/innkeepers:

    Jackson and Marian Taylor-Beatty

    Route 1, Box 136A

    Charlevoix, MI 49720

    (616) 599-2570

Bed and Breakfast of Ludington
Ludington

Grace and Robert Schneider's home is nestled on fifteen acres in Good Creek Valley, just four miles from Ludington. It is surrounded by seventy acres of state land, and it is a paradise for people seeking the rest and relaxation that comes with spending time in the out-of-doors. The Schneiders' home is comfortable and nicely furnished, but, said Robert, "The real beauty is outside these walls." On a warm summer afternoon, he loaned us each a cap and took us for a walk.

We started across the street through a forest of mature beech and conifers, following Good Creek, which ran crystal clear over a sandy bottom. I took off my shoes and waded for several yards—it was years since I had enjoyed that most delectable pleasure. Later, we headed up through the meadow behind the house to a ridge that overlooks the valley. From that vantage, it is easy to see how the area is well protected from northerly winds. That protection and the abundance of fresh water were also appreciated by the Potawatami who settled there in the 1800s.

During the summer, there are black and red raspberries for the picking, as well as strawberries, currants, and blueberries. Robert showed us a series of small ponds, fed by Good Creek, that he keeps stocked with Rocky Mountain spotted rainbow trout. There is a picnic area, plenty of room for outdoor games, and good bird-watching. In winter, toboggans and snowshoes are available for guests to use at no additional charge, and cross-country skis may be rented nearby. There is also a Jacuzzi to soak away any last cares.

The Schneiders enjoy having families visit. Children are welcome and a crib is available. A full breakfast is served daily. Snacks and hot and cold drinks are usually offered during the day. In addition to their innkeeping responsibilities, Grace is a nurse and Robert is part lumberjack, carpenter, mason, and gardener. They are a warm, earnest couple, and they enjoy sharing the pleasures of Good Creek Valley.

Vitals

rooms: 4 that share 3 baths

pets: by arrangement

pets in residence: 1 cat, not allowed in sleeping rooms

smoking: outside only

open season: year-round

rates: $40, $45, and $50 double; $7 less for a single; $6 per extra
occupant in same room

rates include: breakfast

owners/innkeepers:
Grace and Robert Schneider
2458 South Beaune Road
Ludington, MI 49431
(616) 843-9768

Brookside Inn
Beulah

When Pam and Kirk Lorenz began creating the Brookside Inn, they used a pretty basic formula. Said Kirk, "We just put in the things we liked and omitted what we disliked!"

You will find that what they like, for example, are king-sized water beds housed in custom-made wooden frames with lovely etched mirrors in the canopy. Some of the beds have softly lighted glass display cases built into the headboards. Then Pam and Kirk added private bathrooms and equipped each with a hair drier, curling iron, and the thickest towels they could find. They also included in each room a remote control TV, a small wood-burning stove, and a built-in Polynesian spa with temperature and water-jet controls. Some even have saunas, steam baths, or tanning solariums!

The rooms are individually decorated around differing themes and

have been given names instead of numbers. In the New Orleans Room, wrought iron window trim and flower boxes give the flavor of old Bourbon Street. The wallpaper in the Garden Room looks like a continuous watercolor painting of flowers; and our Polynesian Room, with its bamboo motif, had a carpeted stair that led to a little inside balcony and the sauna. There were lots of pretty pillows trimmed with lace and ribbons, and fabric-covered hatboxes of all sizes—very classy and very complete.

About the only reason for guests to leave their rooms is for meals, but Kirk and Pam have taken care of that, too. The main floor of the inn is a restaurant furnished with antiques and all manner of country memorabilia. Large windows at the back of the dining room look out onto a tree-sheltered wooden patio surrounded by quiet Eden Brook and nestled among tall wildflowers. It is a favored spot for dining during pleasant weather, and it is frequently visited by small wildlife looking for leftovers. Beyond the deck are herb gardens from which come many of the seasonings for the daily fare.

The food is innovative and very good. We were especially intrigued with the "stone dinner." A square stone, which, incidentally, comes from a quarry at the base of the Matterhorn, is heated to 700 degrees

and comes to the table with a cut of beef or veal, boneless chicken breast, two shrimps, and three sauces. Kirk showed us how to cook on the stone so the outside of the food is seared and the inside remains tender hot. Also tasty were the veal parmesan, the Brookside's home-made pasta with red sauce, and spicy ribs. Ask for a tour of the new wine cellar. The Lorenzes make an annual trek to Europe to taste and buy. They carry a large variety from French and German vineyards and you can sample them before ordering.

The restaurant is open to the public all day, and baked goods produced from the kitchen long before sunup can be purchased from a glass case in the lobby. All of the food is homemade "from scratch." Overnight guests check in early enough to partake of dinner, which is included with the room, as is a full off-the-menu breakfast.

In 1983, Kirk and Pam opened the Hotel Frankfort, a lovely Victorian-style structure in its namesake city, with accommodations similar to those at the Brookside. It, too, has a good restaurant, and a wine cellar with a dining area. Reservations for either inn may be made by calling the Brookside. Pam and Kirk can also set you up with a hot-air balloon ride. They launch from just behind Eden Brook.

"We've had a lot of great experiences in our travels and lots of good memories," said Kirk. "We try to do the same for our guests here."

Vitals

rooms: 15 with private bath, Polynesian spa, king-sized canopied water bed; rooms with saunas, steam baths, and tanning solariums also available

pets: no

pets in residence: none

smoking: yes

open season: year-round

rates: $165 through $255

rates include: dinner and breakfast for 2, all taxes and tips; alcohol *not* included

owners/innkeepers:

Kirk and Pam Lorenz
115 North Michigan Avenue
Beulah, MI 49617
(616) 882-7271

Chimney Corners
Frankfort

Chimney Corners has been a Rogers family operation from the very beginning. The Rogers brothers came to the Crystal Lake area about 1910. They were partners in the Piqua Handle Company and bought up forty- and eighty-acre parcels of land to log the hardwood. They were particularly fond of a large wooded tract of land that bordered the north shore of the lake, so they built a log cabin there. During the Depression, they moved onto the land permanently, added rooms to the cabin, and began to take in boarders. Mother Rogers's family had been involved with resorts in the Poconos so innkeeping came easy to her. As business increased, the men built a cottage on the property and rented it, then they built another . . . today there are eighteen!

Son Jim and his wife Mollie took over the running of Chimney

Corners during the 1950s. Their daughter, Claudia, and her husband Rick Herman now do much of the work assisted by *their* children.

You cannot see the old log lodge from the highway, but it is easily reached by following a winding wooded road, well-marked on Crystal Drive. The lodge is still in daily use throughout the summer, and in the oldest section you can see the original time-worn-smooth log walls. The main floor has a cozy sitting room loaded with books and two lovely dining rooms that serve some of the best food around. Diners are offered the difficult choice of such items as duck à l'orange, charbroiled rib eye steaks, and broiled whitefish served amid the warmth of stone fireplaces and family tradition. Simple country fare! The restaurant is open to the public, and its success over the years prompted Mollie to publish a cookbook called *There's Always Something Cooking at Chimney Corners,* now in its second edition.

On the second floor of the lodge are small, cottagelike sleeping rooms with dormers and rough wood walls. The furnishings are simple and comfortable with here and there an occasional brass bed or hand-

some wooden dresser. Guests in the eight rooms share two bathrooms.

On the main floor, accessible from a separate entrance, is a small apartment with a private bath, a fireplace, and a great view of the lake. I lost count of the number of fireplaces in the lodge but did learn that the innkeepers' Aunt Nancy built several of them—as well as many of those in the eighteen cottages and five lakeside apartments.

Breakfast and lunch are served at the beach dining room located on a narrow strip of land between the road and Crystal Lake. It is very casual and offers a spectacular and weather-protected view of the water and Chimney Corners' thousand feet of beach.

Vitals

rooms: 9 in lodge; 8 rooms share 2 baths; 1 room has a private bath, large sitting area and a fireplace; also available are 18 cottages and 5 apartments

pets: up to discretion of innkeeper

pets in residence: none

smoking: lodge, preferably outside and on porches; cabins, yes

open season: May through October

rates: $32 through $72

rates include: use of beach and tennis facilities

owners/innkeepers:

Mollie and Jim Rogers
Claudia and Rick Herman
1602 Crystal Drive
Frankfort, MI 49635   S w -7ravcc·c (it,
(616) 352-7522

E. E. Douville Bed and Breakfast
Manistee

Barbara and Bill Johnson bought their big home on Pine Street in 1978, just a year from its one hundredth birthday. It was built by E. E. Douville, a wealthy businessman from Wisconsin who made his money in insurance and real estate. According to Bill, Douville's name appeared frequently in the society columns of the local paper, and he liked to "hobnob with all the lumber barons." He also served as mayor of the town for at least one term. But in the late 1880s, Douville left the area, and little is known about his later years.

It was Douville's generous use of pine woodwork that first attracted Barb and Bill to the house. All the windows and doors on the main floor are trimmed in wide pine boards with elaborate spoon carvings. Original interior pine shutters cover many of the windows. A graceful wind-

ing stairway in the two-story foyer leads to the three sleeping rooms for guests on the second floor.

We stayed in the spacious front room with its tall, shuttered windows that give an air of elegance. Like the other two sleeping rooms, it is beautifully decorated with plush carpeting, country prints, antiques, and a cozy bed quilt. Collections of escutcheon plates and old kitchen tools provide a glimpse of the kinds of items that might have been around when Douville first built his home.

At the end of the hall, past the sleeping rooms, is a combination kitchen, eating area, and sitting room for overnight guests. It is furnished with white wicker and is a quiet and pleasant place to read or sit and talk with other guests. In the morning, it is set up for breakfast: fresh fruit and juice in the refrigerator, coffee or a choice of teas, and some of the best muffins we have ever eaten. The shared bath just off the kitchen has a deep footed tub adapted with a shower.

Barb and Bill maintain the first floor of the home for their own living quarters and are happy to show it to guests. Its extensive pine trim will increase your appreciation for the skills of the wood-carvers who worked on E. E. Douville's home a century ago. Within walking

distance of this home are the 1903 Ramsdell Opera House and the Manistee Historical Museum. Lake Michigan is not far, and with it, fishing and boating. Charter fishing trips and tours can be arranged on the *Pro-Ducer* with its captain, the Johnsons' son Jerry P. Johnson, who is licensed by the U.S. Coast Guard. Barbara also recommends taking a ride on the new trolley that offers a one-hour tour of the area.

Vitals

rooms: 3 sleeping rooms that share 1 bath

pets: no

pets in residence: none

smoking: yes

open season: year-round

rates: $35 through $40 per room

rate includes: Continental breakfast

owners/innkeepers:

William and Barbara Johnson
111 Pine Street
Manistee, MI 49660
(616) 723-8654

Fireside Inn
Alpena

> During the years of 1906 and 1907 my mother and father boarded a group of men who were lumbering Whiskey Point. She fed from 18 to 20 men three meals a day for $3 per week and did this for two years.
>
> Mother saved $350 and started to talk to dad about building a summer hotel. Dad wasn't enthused, as his brother Joe had the Birch Hill Hotel and he did not want to compete with him. But mother and I kept at it and he finally consented to build one.
>
> The only money we had was that $350 . . . but there was lots of timber around and a portable mill at the south end of the lake. We had it ready June 22, 1909. We had eight rooms upstairs and charged $10 per week for room and board. That was big money at the time. When we opened the hotel . . . our $350 was gone but everything was paid. We didn't owe one dime. It was named the Fireside Inn because it had the second fireplace at Grand Lake.*

. . . and so began the first of decades of summer lodging at the Fireside Inn, tucked along the east shore of Grand Lake north of Alpena. Kauffman, quoted above, eventually bought the inn from his father and kept it until 1945. During the next thirty years, it changed ownership only a couple of times before Lois and Bob McConnell made their way north from the Detroit suburb of Warren and bought the inn in 1975.

The resort sprawls over seventeen acres and has 700 feet of frontage on Grand Lake. There is a lot to do if you want to be outside and active, and plenty of places to cozy yourself away if you do not. Porch sitting is a great pastime at the Fireside Inn, and oh, what a porch! As the Kauffman's business increased, father and son had added a wing of rooms to the east end of the lodge, running parallel to the lake, and they extended the wide, covered porch the full length of the wing. It is nearly 215 feet long and is now shaded by huge old cedar trees that appear as twigs in a photograph taken sometime during 1912. The sleeping rooms that open onto the porch are simply furnished with a

---

*From *My Recollections of Early Grand Lake* by George H. Kauffman. In the early 1970s George Kauffman began writing stories of early Grand Lake life in letters to his grandchildren. Son-in-law Lew Sowa encouraged him to write more, with the thought of compiling the memories in a small book so they would not be lost. The first edition, written with colorful and tender firsthand details, was released in 1973. Three months later, Mr. Kauffman died. We are most grateful to Mr. Sowa for permission to reprint from the book.

bed or two, a dresser, and chairs. They also have screened doors for letting in the balmy lake breezes. Last year, Bob and Lois opened ten small guest rooms on the second floor of the lodge that are carpeted and share two full baths.

Between 1940 and 1945, George Kauffman built eighteen cabins on the Fireside grounds. Sixteen of varying sizes house summer guests and are furnished similarly to the lodge rooms: casual and homey. Each has a refrigerator and some come with complete cooking facilities. All but one has at least one stone fireplace.

The Fireside Room in the lodge is one of the favored gathering places. The walls are finished in half logs and are covered with historic paraphernalia and old mounted birds and mammals from the area. Most of the items have been in the room for a very long time . . . passed on from owner to owner. A player piano sits in one corner with a stack of rolls that would take a week to go through. On cool days and nights, a fire is usually ablaze in the namesake hearth. If not, guests are welcome to build one. The inn is comfortably rustic, and guests seem drawn to it, says Lois, because it is safe, quiet, and easy to get-away-from-it-all.

Breakfast and dinner are served to guests in July and August. Local residents often make reservations and come in for dinner too. A differ-

ent item is served each night, rotating such features as spaghetti, chicken, and whitefish. The roast pork supper we feasted on was delicious, and we topped it off with ice cream and homemade strawberry shortcake. Breakfast was any combination of cold or hot cereal, French toast, pancakes, eggs, sausage, juice, and coffee—plenty of food to keep guests fueled for hours.

Canoes, paddleboats, and small sailboats are available to guests at all times. Boats with motors are rented for a small fee. Guests may also bring their own. On-land facilities include a tennis court and horseshoe pit, a volleyball court, and wooded walking trails.

Vitals

rooms: 16 cabins with bathrooms; 5 sleeping rooms in lodge wing, each with private bath; 10 second-floor lodge rooms that share 2 full baths

pets: by prior arrangement

pets in residence: 1 cat

smoking: yes

open season: Memorial Day through Labor Day

rates: $23 through $35 daily per adult for rooms; $200 per adult by the week for cottages; special rates for children and for off-season lodging, including Memorial Day, Labor Day, and fall color weekends

rates include: breakfast and dinner from mid-June through August, use of all outdoor equipment except boats with motors

owners/innkeepers:

Bob and Lois McConnell
18730 Fireside Highway
Alpena, MI 49707
(517) 595-6369

The House on the Hill
Ellsworth

Buster and Julie Arnim sold their interest in a Houston-based luggage company a few years ago and decided that running a bed-and-breakfast home would suit them well. They made a list of about eight features they would look for, among them a location in a resort region near fresh water and close to excellent dining. A reference to northern Michigan and its resemblance to the beautiful Hudson River Valley piqued their interest in the Great Lakes State. And when they came across an ad for a farmhouse on fifty-three and a half acres in Ellsworth, they put in an offer. It was accepted, and they closed without ever having set foot in Michigan. Their first look at the area came the following January, when Ellsworth lay under five feet of snow. Julie remembers walking through the house repeating, "I love it, I love it, I love it!" It was a gutsy move, she admits. But it has worked out just fine.

As its name implies, the house sits on a hill and overlooks a valley through which flows Lake St. Clair, part of the Chain of Lakes. The Arnims' renovation work included adding a large veranda that wraps around two sides of the house and forms a gazebo at the corner. The view from that veranda, out across the lush valley to the sparkling wa-

ter and rolling landscape of this resort area, is spectacular. The three second-floor guest rooms face the lake and have windows that take advantage of the view.

The home is decorated with a country Victorian theme, elegant but casual, with touches of art from the American West. Many of the walls are framed in beautiful border papers that set off a very comfortable blend of period furnishings. The sleeping rooms are filled with the kinds of amenities that Buster and Julie have enjoyed in their travels to bed-and-breakfast homes and have incorporated for the pleasure of their own guests. Among them are end tables and reading lights on each side of the bed, a carafe of ice water, and a plate (a whole plate!) of chocolate mints.

Within easy walking distance of the House on the Hill are two of northern Michigan's premier restaurants, the Rowe Inn and Tapawingo. If good food is what brings you to the area, save room for Buster and Julie's country breakfasts. They vary throughout the year. You may, for example, find yourself feasting one morning on a spicy Tex-Mex breakfast, and the next day on a baked apple pancake served with sugar, butter, and cinnamon, topped with sour cream and maple syrup.

Be prepared here for bountiful quantities of Texas hospitality— there are few things quite as endearing—and for two delightful people who adore each other. There is laughter here, and warmth and good memory-making. We can agree with the feeling Buster expressed one summer evening as dusk was settling into the valley while we sipped wine on the veranda: "It doesn't get any better than this."

Vitals

rooms: 3 that share 1 bath

pets: no

pets in residence: 1 cat and 1 dog, not allowed in guest rooms

smoking: on porch only

open season: mid-April through January 1

rate: $60 per room

rate includes: full breakfast, tax

owners/innkeepers:
   Julie and Buster Arnim
   Box 206, Lake Street
   Ellsworth, MI 49729
   (616) 588-6304

Leelanau Country Inn
Maple City

The Leelanau Country Inn is located about eight miles south of the town of Leland and just across the road from Little Traverse Lake. The original structure was built in 1891 and served as a stop for travelers needing food and rest. An addition was put on in 1895 and the clientele began to shift to vacationers who came to the area for summer recreation.

There is a peacefulness that has settled over this rural area and that wavers only slightly even during the busiest tourist seasons. John and Linda Sisson think that is one of the best reasons to come visit. They bought the inn and opened it in May, 1984. John worked for the Chuck Muer restaurants for several years and Linda was a longtime employee of Leland's well-known Blue Bird Restaurant. Their combined talents produced a blending of competent service and superb food, with a backdrop of beautiful country decor—all of which made the inn an overnight success.

John is unrelenting in his quest to serve the best. "We offer at least twenty appetizers and fifty entrées, and the entire menu is printed daily to assure the freshest possible products available," he explained. The fish is flown in from the three North American coasts and the linguini is homemade. Every plate that comes out of the kitchen is arranged and garnished as though it was prepared as the subject of an artist's still life. We ate heartily . . . and even in the interest of thorough research, there wasn't room for a single bite of peach pudding, strawberry shortcake, or cherry cobbler.

Although the emphasis here is on the restaurant, like a traditional country inn, there are sleeping rooms available on the second floor.

Four are very spacious—large enough to make yourself at home for a few days while you explore the peninsula. The others are small but pretty and comfortable. All are decorated around the country theme, and when we visited in June there were green plants and freshly cut flowers in many of them.

Overnight guests are treated to croissants, muffins, and fresh fruit in the morning, as well as marvelous waftings from the kitchen while Linda, John, and their skilled staff prepare for another day at the inn.

Vitals

rooms: 10 second-floor sleeping rooms that share 2 bathrooms on the second floor and 2 restrooms with sink and toilet on the first floor

pets: ask the innkeeper

pets in residence: none

smoking: not allowed in sleeping rooms; OK in restaurant

open season: year-round

rates: $35 through $45, add $5 per child

rates include: Continental breakfast

owners/innkeepers:
John and Linda Sisson
149 East Harbor Highway (M-22)
Maple City, MI 49664
(616) 228-5060

Neahtawanta Inn
Traverse City (Bowers Harbor)

In some ways, Neahtawanta has not changed much from its early days of this century when it was called the Sunrise Inn, or its pre–World War II year as the Ne Ah Ta Wanta Hotel. Sitting high on a bluff overlooking Bowers Harbor, guests came for the area's natural resources, the beaches and clean water, and the beauty of the surrounding woods. There was good food and fellowship, and the kind of deep sleep that comes from days filled with fresh air and activity.

Since the early 1980s, the Neahtawanta Inn has offered friends and casual travelers more than just a piece of the north country. It began as the focal point of a quiet movement, a group of individuals interested in bettering the environment, themselves, and as much of the world around them as they could touch. The goal was to create a place where people could come together to share problems and resolve conflict in close proximity to nature. It was a stopover for restless philosophers of

the 1960s and 1970s hoping to make sense out of the 1980s. We have watched it gradually evolve.

As was the dream of its guiding forces, Neahtawanta hosts individuals seeking rest and retreat, as well as environmental workshops, women's gatherings, and small groups debating the issues of the day. The inn also houses the Neahtawanta Research and Education Center, a non-profit organization that focuses on "peace, community, sustainable use of resources, and personal growth issues." There is an atmosphere of good health and harmony, reinforced by innkeepers Sally Van Vleck and Bob Russell; David Krumlauf, the resident baker; and Moksha, who is a certified massage therapist. Sally's three daughters are on hand to help with the daily operations of the inn and provide babysitting.

For overnight guests, there are four sleeping rooms on the second floor furnished with antique beds and dressers, many of which have been at the inn since its early days. Two of the rooms have original washbasins with marble counters. Recent renovations have produced a more contemporary third-floor dormer suite available for a family or small group of up to six. Its two small sleeping rooms are furnished with Japanese futons. Guests in the suite share a common area and a private outside entrance with a deck. The first floor is large and open

with plenty of sitting areas, shelves full of books, and a massive sunken fieldstone fireplace.

A Continental breakfast of whole wheat croissants, whole wheat coffee cakes or muffins, juice, coffee, and tea is served family style around the big dining room table. Additional meals may be provided for groups by special arrangement.

Sally leads a weekly yoga class and will teach it on request. There is a wood-burning sauna for guests' enjoyment, and the swimming here is excellent.

Vitals

rooms: 6 sleeping rooms; 4 share 1 bath, 2 sleeping rooms with suite share 1 bath

pets: up to discretion of innkeepers

pets in residence: 1 cat and 1 dog

smoking: no

open season: year-round

rates: begin at $40 single, $50 double; suite from $90 for a family, $100 for two couples, additional persons each $10; entire inn $250 to $330 per night

rates include: Continental breakfast

owners/innkeepers:
Sally Van Vleck and Bob Russell
1308 Neahtawanta Road
Traverse City, MI 49684
(616) 223-7315

North Shore Inn
Northport

Sue and Dick Hammersley's North Shore Inn is tucked along the sandy edge of Grand Traverse Bay. If you look at a map of the Leelanau Peninsula, you will see that Northport sits inside a tiny bay within Grand Traverse, offering a protected harbor of refuge.

This home was part of a former estate developed in 1945. When Dick and Sue bought it in 1983, they radically remodeled it with a focus on Colonial decor. A few years later, Sue left her job as a preschool teacher and, with the blessings of the family, turned their lovely lakeside home into a luxurious retreat for bed-and-breakfast travelers.

"Bed and breakfast has been very successful in Northport," Sue explained, "and I knew this was a good house to share."

Four guest rooms are available including the Heritage Room that will accommodate a family of four or two couples. Located on the main floor for easy access, it has a complete kitchen and private entrance with a tree-shaded patio. The spacious Country Rose Room is the most frequent choice of honeymooners and guests celebrating special occa-

sions. It has a romantic, pink marble fireplace for chilly nights and a private balcony that overlooks the bay.

The nautical motif in the Ships Room includes a library of books on the Great Lakes. The view to the east takes in Sue's English-style garden from which she harvests many of the herbs and flowers you will find throughout the home. Carla's Room is the smallest of the four, though equally well-appointed with Early American furnishings including an antique walnut bed and matching chest. It is the only guest room without a private bath and is used only when a family or two parties traveling together want two rooms.

Sue serves wine and hors d'oeuvres in the late afternoon and encourages her guests to make themselves at home. A large bay floor-to-ceiling window in the living room offers an exceptional view of the lake. There is also a fireplace to snuggle by and a piano and organ for the musically inclined.

Sue serves a generous sit-down breakfast every morning and varies the menu to fit the season. There is always fresh fruit and juice accompanied by a selection of muffins, coffee cake or cobblers, and an entrée usually made with eggs from organically raised chickens. Depending on

the weather, it may be served in the big dining room or the screened porch. Guests may also request that it be brought to their rooms.

Dick owns the Northport Construction Company. He is also an accomplished furniture maker and you will see his handiwork around the inn. He and Sue are genial hosts and good tour guides, having lived in the Northport area for twenty years. You can rely on their recommendations for restaurants and points of interest.

Vitals

rooms: 4, 3 have a private bath, the 4th room is available to 2 couples or a family wishing to occupy 2 rooms.

pets: no

pets in residence: none

smoking: yes, with courteous consideration

open season: May through October, winter weekends on request

rates: $75 through $85 double occupancy

rates include: breakfast, beverages, hors d'oeuvres, use of bicycles and beach

owners/innkeepers:
Sue and Dick Hammersley
12794 County Road 640
Northport, MI 49670
(616) 386-7111

note: The 1989 season is the last that the Hammersleys expect they will operate their North Shore Inn. Ask about their plans to open Indian Beach Country Inn in summer, 1990.

The Old Mill Pond Inn
Northport

David Chrobak's home is reached by a short winding driveway that, in late July, was edged with a profusion of snapdragons, salvia, dahlias, cosmos, and petunias. It gave us the first indication of David's talent with flowers and a hint at the work he has put into plantings throughout the estate. The entire inn was rimmed in perennials. Black-eyed Susans, daisies, and lilies were mixed with annuals of all colors. A rose garden bordered a small parking area, and beyond it was yet another garden enclosed with a fence made of small, unpeeled tree limbs. Flower

baskets hung from every porch and encircled a gazebo that David designed and built. By far, the most spectacular of his creations is a huge side garden with four larger than life-size statues of Neptune, Bacchus, Venus, and one of the seasons keeping watch. A Greek column stands in the center.

David has lived on St. Thomas, in the Virgin Islands, since 1969. He operates a flower and gift shop there, but as the island's summer season is slow, he decided to return to his home state and set up a summer residence. He wanted a big house but thought it was senseless to have so much room all to himself. A friend opened a bed-and-breakfast home in upstate New York, and David was inspired to follow suit. His inn was built as a summer cottage for the Carmen family in 1895. For the first

several decades, the interior walls were covered with tar paper nailed to the studs. In 1952, they were finished off with pine paneling. Walking through the parlor and the dining room, you will see that the inn is filled with the handpicked treasures of a well-traveled innkeeper. David's collections of tiny picture frames, crystal and copper, Marilyn Monroe memorabilia, and many other wonderful things adorn the walls and are tucked in numerous glass-fronted cabinets. They fill shelves and are arranged on sideboards, mingling with twentieth-century masters and primitive Peruvian tapestry. David's love of the whimsical is apparent in various pottery pieces and in the appearance of an occasional pink flamingo. During our stay, there were tall jardinieres everywhere, filled with flowers and greenery. It was like walking into a private museum.

Sleeping rooms are on the second and third floors. Feeling that guests seldom use dressers and chests of drawers, David left them out and put comfortable chairs and a sitting area in each room instead. The styles and periods of the furnishings vary throughout the house. Some are more formal, as with the polished dining room set, others casual. The large wraparound porch has several wicker tables and chairs for relaxing and taking in the cool lake breezes. You may be joined by Muffy, David's Westie, or the more shy Molly, a Scottie.

Among his many talents, David is an accomplished cook. Our breakfast began with individual plates of fruit artistically arranged. They were followed by chicken crepes and whole cherry tomatoes sautéed with herbs. On other mornings, David's guests might be treated to eggs with herbs and mushrooms, or a vegetable quiche. For a pleasant stroll after breakfast, head down the hill toward town and visit David's shop, "Important Pieces."

David feels he may be looked on as the town eccentric, a title that makes him smile. He rather likes it. His life is full and exciting, and the Old Mill Pond Inn is a reflection of his joie de vivre.

Vitals

rooms: 5 that share 3 baths

pets: no

pets in residence: 2 dogs

smoking: yes

open season: June 1 through November 1

rates: $65 double occupancy, roll-away beds $10

rate includes: full breakfast from 8 A.M. to 9 A.M., Continental breakfast after 9 A.M.

owner/innkeeper:
David Chrobak
202 West 3rd Street
Northport, MI 49670
(616) 386-7341

winter address:
23 Store Tvaer Gade
St. Thomas, U.S. Virgin Islands 00802

Plum Lane Inn
Northport

Beatrice Bowen opened her country Victorian home as a bed-and-breakfast inn in 1982. From their vantage point, tucked in the wooded hillside that overlooks Grand Traverse Bay, Plum Lane's guests get a lovely slice of Northport life.

"The bed-and-breakfast concept is great for travelers," Bea explained. "Heretofore, we've invited visitors and allowed them to just see. With bed and breakfast, we allow them to get involved and feel— people experience another life-style. Over breakfast coffee, conversation is a stimulating part of the B & B experience."

Bea received a Ph.D. from the University of Michigan, and for the past several years she has been an outspoken and respected educator on the teaching of children's literature. When she retired from her position as a coordinator in the Livonia school system and moved to Northport, her schedule quickly filled with speaking engagements and meetings with special interest groups. But she saved enough time for a

few less intense activities such as the care and feeding of her chickens, gardening, and innkeeping. When we spoke last fall, Bea proudly announced that the Thumb-area Organic Association had, after inspection, declared her a certified organic gardener.

Plum Lane is beautifully furnished with graceful Victorian accents and reading material that fills a full wall of bookshelves. The three upstairs sleeping rooms are spacious and bright. One has a private screened porch with a treetop view of the bay and an extra sleeping alcove. Guests are invited to join their hostess for an elegant breakfast, most often served in the formal dining room, accompanied by fine china and crystal.

Plum Lane is a great place to unwind for a few days and elude the madness of routine. It is also within easy driving distance of shops, restaurants, and the peninsula's year-round outdoor recreational areas.

Vitals

rooms: 3 with private baths

pets: no

pets in residence: 1 cat and 1 dog, not allowed in guest rooms

smoking: outside and on porches only

open season: spring, summer, and fall

rates: $65 through $70

rates include: breakfast

owner/innkeeper:

Beatrice Bowen
Box 74
Northport, MI 49670
(616) 386-5774

Stafford's Bay View Inn
Petoskey

Late in the 1950s, Stafford Smith was working his way through the ranks at an inn on the edge of the Bay View community. The building had been constructed in 1886 on property leased from the Bay View Association and was owned at the time of Stafford's employment by Dr. Roy Heath. It offered fifty-eight second- and third-floor rooms to guests from July 4 through Labor Day.

In the fall of 1960, Dr. Heath actively sought to sell the inn. Stafford, meanwhile, was about to marry Janice, the inn's hostess, and was actively seeking full-time work. The following spring, Stafford approached Dr. Heath about buying the business and they struck an easy deal. Many of the Smiths' early guests were widows or widowers who came up to stay two, three, and even four weeks while attending the Bay View cultural programs. Stafford remembers when vacationers could arrive in Petoskey from Cincinnati by train.

During the past twenty-five years, the inn has undergone several redecorations and rebuildings with each one more elegant and accom-

modating than the last. Antiques and wicker, bold fabrics, and richly colored wallpaper give the inn a well-seasoned country look and a feeling of homelike comfort and permanence. Manager Judy Honor oversaw renovation of the spacious third-floor rooms and suites that were opened in May, 1987. Their sophisticated furnishings include canopy and king-sized four-poster beds. Guests will find such special touches as pincushion baskets with needles and thread, a thick folder filled with information about the inn and the Bay View–Petoskey community, and handmade eyelet and ribbon pillows. Stafford thought parents would like to be able to put their children to bed and leave the room but still be close enough to hear them call, so he added a handsome sitting room on the third floor that serves the purpose well.

The lovely main-floor dining rooms are bright and airy, and Stafford can often be found mingling among the tables greeting friends. The inn's well-deserved reputation for good food reflects years of recipe perfecting and the Smiths' ongoing concern for quality. Many of the selections are reminiscent of what turn-of-the-century guests might have enjoyed, such as steaming bread pudding with raisins and cream. Sunday brunch is a special affair at the inn. With Stafford at the helm carving ham and turkey, guests help themselves to a bountiful buffet

that, during our vist, included eggs, chicken and biscuits, whitefish, fruits, breads and muffins, waffles, pots of Rocky Top Farms preserves, bite-sized portions of desserts, and much more. The inn does not serve alcoholic beverages, but houseguests are welcome to bring a bottle of wine to dinner.

Guests are greeted and assisted by a staff that we found to be— without exception—friendly, happy, and very helpful. Among them is Judy Honor who has been in innkeeping all her professional life.

Stafford's Bay View welcomes children and is well equipped to handle them. On the morning of one of our visits, Janice had purchased another crib to be sure she had enough available for the number of young families that stay at the inn. Stafford explained the perfect setup, "When children get restless at the dinner table, they can climb down from their chairs and play in the common rooms of the inn, which are pretty kid proof, leaving Mom and Dad to enjoy a leisurely meal."

"One of the elements so necessary to the country inn feeling is getting to know the guests," added Stafford. "I love the interplay we have with them. They enjoy being part of historic America, and it's nice to be here and be part of that feeling."

Vitals

rooms: 30 with private baths

pets: no

pets in residence: none

smoking: yes

open season: year-round

rates: $48 through $75 single, $60 through $105 double; $120 through $140 for suites

rates include: full breakfast from the menu

owners:
   Stafford and Janice Smith

innkeepers:
   Stafford and Janice Smith
   Judy Honor
   US 31 North
   Petoskey, MI 49770
   (616) 347-2771

The Sylvan Inn
Glen Arbor

There is something about rocking chairs on a covered porch that is as good as hanging out the Welcome sign. Add warm, sophisticated decor, handpicked furnishings, and rooms that are as accommodating as they are spotlessly clean. Surround it all with a century of history and the mysterious Sleeping Bear Dunes National Lakeshore, and you have the elements of this fine country inn.

Proprietors Joe and Sue Williamson have lived in the area for fourteen years and are keenly aware of the natural resources that abound in their corner of the state. Joe, in fact, first fell in love with the area when he was a student at the Leelanau Schools.

Their 100-year-old inn was originally a house converted for lodging in the early 1900s to serve the lumbermen and sailors of the day. By 1940, it was on its way through a series of different owners and uses, and eventually became an antique shop. When it came up for sale in 1986, Joe and Sue bought the building, contents and all. It was a natural choice to turn it back into an inn. Said Joe, "We wanted to give some-

thing back to the community that had given us so much enjoyment."

There are two distinct parts to the new Sylvan Inn and great variety in the accommodations. The original structure houses seven completely renovated and refurbished sleeping rooms. They are decorated around a country theme with pretty fabrics and furnishings gleaned from the antique shop inventory. Each has a convenient corner sink typical of old inns. They share three baths and have the use of a cozy parlor.

For guests wishing more deluxe accommodations, the Williamsons added six rooms in the adjacent, attached Great House that are fully carpeted and have a bolder, more contemporary look. Each has a TV, phone, and private bath. Several have sun decks from which you can see Lake Michigan and the dunes. There is also a suite that will sleep four adults and comes complete with a "demi-kitchen" that is a perfect arrangement for extended stays. One room and bath are barrier-free. Sue selected linens by British designer Laura Ashley for many of the rooms, along with thick bath towels that will wrap you in softness. At the end of the day, guests can visit the glassed-in spa and relax in the large whirlpool or take a sauna.

Breakfast here includes a choice of pastries, fruit, and beverages. When the inn is full, breakfast is served buffet-style in the first-floor lobby-parlor. But if you visit in the off-season, Joe has a little more time to give individual attention to the guests, and you may find it delivered right to your room. Joe can direct you to a footpath that will lead you to the lake and the dunes in just a couple minutes. Check out the gift and clothing stores along Glen Arbor's main street, too, including Sue's shop, the Black Swan, that specializes in resort wear and distinctive jewelry.

Vitals

rooms: 14, 7 with private baths, 3 that share 1 bath, 4 that share 2 baths

pets: no

pets in residence: none

smoking: outside only

open season: mid-May through ski season

rates: $50 through $110, double occupancy, $12 per extra person

rates include: Continental breakfast

owners/innkeepers:
Joe and Sue Williamson
6680 Western Avenue (M-109)
Glen Arbor, MI 49636
(616) 334-4333

The Terrace Inn
Bay View

In 1875, the Methodist Church established the Bay View Assembly on a hilly, 430-acre plot of land overlooking Little Traverse Bay. It was part of the Chautauqua movement, which provided facilities for intellectual and scientific study, music and the arts, and emphasized religion and morality. At the turn of the century, as many as 3,000 people often attended the Bay View Sunday service. Hundreds of summer homes were built on the acreage in the late nineteenth and early twentieth centuries with elaborate architecture, the likes of which will probably never be duplicated. As sections of land were designated for specific purposes, a plot of ground was set aside for commercial lodging. In 1911, Bay View residents celebrated the opening of the Terrace Inn.

For years, the inn was a popular destination for the overflow of guests at the nearby cottages and for elderly Bay View residents who no

longer wanted to maintain a big summer home. The accommodations were spartan, though impeccably clean, and the food was good.

In 1986, innkeepers Pat and Mary Lou Barbour oversaw a skillful renovation of the inn. They completely and individually redecorated forty-four sleeping rooms and gave each a private bath. They brought in new beds, added country French wallpaper prints, and outfitted the larger rooms with sitting areas. You do not have to be shy about wanting to see the variety that is available. "The doors are left open to unoccupied rooms," Pat explained, "so visitors can stroll the halls and take a look."

The warm, elegant lobby and dining room have deep green and plum furnishings that complement the original, hemlock-paneled walls. There is a spectacular rose-and-vine wallpaper in the dining room that enhances the height of the beamed ceiling while little glass lamps on the room's wooden columns create a festive glow.

Our dinner of planked whitefish with duchess potatoes was, quite simply, excellent. It was accompanied by hot bread and fresh vegetables, preceded by crisp salad, and—despite our claims of being "stuffed"—followed by a memorable ice cream eclair. The menu has

many other tempting items including Lobster Alfredo, chicken stir-fry, baked lasagna, and a fresh catch of the day. An early dinner menu, available between 5 P.M. and 6 P.M. offers several light entrées at a special price.

Breakfast and lunch are also served through the summer. Standard favorites are available along with some unexpected treats such as a walnut chicken salad and a California burger with guacamole. Save room for mud pie, brownie bottom pie, or hot fudge cake. Or stop by the old-fashioned ice cream parlor in the lower level and try one of the fountain specialties.

Most of the dwellings in Bay View are occupied just in the summer; in the winter only one road is plowed free of snow. "Winter is a lovely time to visit," Pat told us. "It's very quiet, and you can cross-country ski throughout Bay View."

You will not find TVs or phones in the rooms. But you will find people talking together. "Many guests rediscover the art of conversation here," said Pat. "And they get the chance to finish the book they started two months earlier."

The inn offers a balance of quiet gentility and vitality that characterizes the Bay View community itself. Of the fifteen such Chautauquas instituted around the country, this is one of only three where the original bylaws are still enforced. And the association still maintains a full program of arts and religion throughout the summer.

Vitals

rooms: 44 with private bath

pets: no

pets in residence: none

smoking: yes

open season: year-round

rates: $62 through $72 double occupancy in summer, substantial discounts before June 17 and after October 16, $10 for a cot or crib, $15 discount for families sharing adjoining rooms with children under 18

rates include: room only

innkeepers:

Patrick and Mary Lou Barbour
216 Fairview
P.O. Box 1478
Bay View, MI 49770
(616) 347-2410

Torch Lake Bed and Breakfast
Alden

Patti Findlay's sweet, Carpenter Gothic bed-and-breakfast home is perched on a hill just a stone's throw from Torch Lake. It was built in 1895 by the Main family. Mr. Main also owned a hotel across the street on the lakeshore, and from his home, he could conveniently keep a close eye on the business. The old hotel is gone now. Like so many turn-of-the century clapboard buildings, it disappeared years ago, leaving an unobstructed view of the lake from the Findlays' front porch. We sat there one quiet summer afternoon and remarked on the beauty and clarity of Torch Lake. The locals, explained Patti, talk about five-color days when the water displays five distinct shades of blue.

It spite of its age and neglected condition, it took little convincing when a friend suggested that Patti buy this house and realize her dream by opening it as a summertime bed-and-breakfast home. After extensive renovation ("Everything had to be replaced!"), Patti gave the home a fresh, country French look with bright cotton prints, lace curtains, and lovely antiques. Some of the furnishings are well-traveled treasures. The

small love seat in the parlor was purchased from a family that decades ago brought it from Ohio to Pennsylvania in a covered wagon.

A handsome new oak stair, handcrafted by a local carpenter, leads to three pretty, second-floor sleeping rooms. We stayed in the Violet Room, which overlooks the lake and has a private bath. It is furnished in summery whites with an iron and brass bed, crisp linens edged with lace and eyelet, and a wicker settee. In the late afternoon, sunlight shines through stained glass windows splashing a rainbow of colors across the wall. On either side of the bed is a soft sheepskin rug, brought from Australia, that is a real barefoot treat first thing in the morning.

The adjacent Trillium Room has twin beds covered with luxurious Irish wool spreads. It shares a full bath with the Primrose Room. All three rooms have ceiling fans for warm summer nights.

When we visited in June, ripe strawberries were just coming to market and we were treated to a dish of Patti's homemade strawberry shortcake before bedtime. The next morning, we awoke to wonderful aromas wafting up from the kitchen. Breakfast was served at 9:00, and we feasted on baked French toast with pecan-praline syrup and Michigan fruit preserves. Patti varies morning entrées and counts among her

specialties oatmeal, raisin scones, and sausage-filled crepes with a buttery cream sauce.

Alden is a tiny, but bustling village. Across the street from the bed and breakfast is the old Alden depot that has been renovated along with a lakeside park. The ice cream parlor at the end of the street and the used bookstore a few doors from the inn are both enjoyable late-afternoon destinations. So is Patti's porch. And in Alden, porch sitting just seems a natural way to pass some time on a summer day.

Vitals

rooms: 3, 1 with a private bath, 2 share 1 full bath

pets: no

pets in residence: none

smoking: outside

open season: Memorial Day through Labor Day

rates: $50 through $60 double occupancy

rates include: breakfast

owners: Jack and Patti Findlay

innkeeper:

    Patti Findlay
    10601 Coy Street
    Alden, MI 49612
    (616) 331-6424

Walloon Lake Inn
Walloon Lake Village

The emphasis at Walloon Lake Inn has, for several years, been the food, and it appears to be splendid. There are several trout dishes, including an appetizer of fillet of brook trout smoked on the premises; venison with a sauce of prosciutto, Madeira, and thyme; breast of chicken with morel sauce; escalope of pork diablo with roasted chilies, tomatoes, and garlic; strawberry almond duck; a daily veal special; and much more. If there is room for dessert, you can try citrons givrel, daily pastries, homemade ice cream, or any of several other sweet-sounding choices. Children are welcome and will find a special menu to suit their tastes.

In 1986 the inn's five second-floor sleeping rooms were completely renovated and redecorated. They are carpeted and furnished with antiques that nicely complement this nearly one-hundred-year-old structure. Guests share a common area that overlooks the lake.

"Most of our guests like to come here to eat, swim, fish, and sit on the dock," said David Beier, innkeeper, chef, and proprietor of Walloon Lake Inn. Last summer he introduced the Windermere, a steam launch that is a near replica of the boats that once populated this lake. It will carry eight to ten passengers and is available for charter.

Cross-country skiing in the area is excellent and the inn offers a special winter package that includes two nights lodging and lots of food. If you want to learn some of the secrets of David's fine cuisine, ask about his four-day Fonds Du Cuisine cooking school. He offers it periodically during the year; enrollment is limited to six students per class.

Vitals

rooms: 5 sleeping with private baths

pets: no

pets in residence: none

smoking: yes

open season: year-round, but closed for two days each week in April

rates: $50.00 double occupancy; dinners $12.50 through $18.00

rates include: Continental breakfast (with room)

owner/innkeeper:
David Beier
P.O. Box 85
Walloon Lake Village, MI 49796
(616) 535-2999

Warwickshire Inn
Traverse City

This stately bed-and-breakfast inn sits atop a long hill just outside Traverse City, affording a spectacular view of the bay to the east. The present structure was built in 1902 by the Barney family, but the front of the home rests on a foundation dating from 1854. The lumber used by Mr. Barney to build this country estate came from a wooded parcel that he owned on Long Lake, about five miles away. Barney had the trees cut and floated down the Boardman River to the Brown Lumber Company.

Barney's primary business was insurance, but he also had the first herd of registered cattle in northern Michigan, and he served as president of the Northwestern Michigan Fair for twenty-five years. His house, for the times, was very modern. Gas lights lit the rooms and a second-

floor water storage tank supplied the first floor, with an overflow that ran out to the barn. The home was surrounded by several acres of fruit trees, earning it the name Orchard Lawn. Much of the nearby land still belongs to the Barney family, and the road retains the family name.

Pat and Dan Warwick bought the homestead in 1976 after Dan retired from a career with the Air Force. They finished raising five children and opened their home as a bed-and-breakfast lodging in October, 1983. The furnishings at Warwickshire are a sophisticated and comfortable blend of the old country and the new. Some of the fine antiques, including an elegant hand-crocheted cover on one of the beds, originally belonged to Dan's grandmother. There are also pieces that the Warwicks brought back from their residences in Germany and England while with the Air Force. They complement handsome old wardrobes, rockers, and dressers with rich patinas and their own inter-esting histories. The warm country feeling is enhanced by the scent of cinnamon and spices that Pat often simmers in a pot on the stove.

Breakfast is elaborate and elegant, served on Wedgwood china with

fine silver service. There again, you will be treated to pleasantries that the Warwicks brought back from their world travels such as coddled eggs and marmalades.

The peacefulness of rural life at Warwickshire belies its actual closeness to Traverse City and all the conveniences of downtown. Sugar Loaf is also just a short drive away, as are beaches and antique shops, cross-country skiing trails, and Interlochen Arts Academy.

Vitals

rooms: 3 rooms with private baths

pets: no, but there is a kennel nearby

pets in residence: 1 Afghan hound, confined to innkeepers' quarters

smoking: yes, in designated areas

open season: year-round

rates: $55 through $65 double occupancy

rates include: breakfast

owners/innkeepers:
    Pat and Dan Warwick
    5037 Barney Road
    Traverse City, MI 49684
    (616) 946-7176

White Rose Country Inn
Ludington

We were enjoying breakfast in the big lakeside dining room, watching the morning mist rise on Hamlin Lake when Terry told us the history of this lovely inn. It was known in the 1940s and 1950s as Sportsmen's Haven, she explained. The inn was advertised as a camp for "gentlemen fishermen only." The owners served two meals daily to guests and maintained a bait shop and confectionary on the premises. Later, it was renamed Tanglewood Lodge.

Dave and Terry bought the building in 1984, just in time to celebrate their second aniversary. They gave the structure a complete facelift, inside and out, and even moved a few walls. Terry has enviable
decorating skills and Dave, it seems, can build or fix anything. Together,
they have transformed the old lodge into the quintessential small country inn with colorful rooms, comfortable furnishings, and a marvelous
deck that overlooks the lake and the Manistee National Forest beyond it.
Vases of flowers, potpourri, dried herbs, and Terry's baking furnish a
medley of subtle, enticing aromas that vary from room to room.

To accommodate their guests' preferences of decor, Terry furnished the seven guest rooms individually. The Nature Room, for example, has two full-sized quarter-canopy beds, tailored in rich, deep
shades of teal and burgundy, and a tiny duck print wallpaper. The
Jennifer Room has a queen-sized canopied bed with mint green and
mauve accessories and access to a private deck.

The first-floor Country Comfort Room has twin beds, a full bath, and a private deck with a lake view. Terry added crisp, floral-patterned, polished cotton linens and a complementing pin-striped wallcovering.

Breakfast is tasty and ample. We enjoyed a fresh fruit salad, Terry's homemade muffins with Michigan-made jellies, and hard-cooked brown eggs. When weather permits, guests can enjoy breakfast on the deck and watch an abundance of birds and wildlife.

There is good swimming right from the dock, and boat slips are available. Let Dave or Terry know in advance if you plan to bring a boat. You can also rent powerboats or paddleboats from a marina that is just a short stroll from the inn. There are plenty of activities available in the area and the Roses can help with with ideas and directions.

If you are looking for an inn with a Christian influence, your visit to the White Rose may be especially enjoyable, because you will share a common bond with Dave and Terry who have a deep, sustaining faith. But there is no pressure here. The Roses' interests range from business and finance to psychology, formula car racing, politics, and flying. You will find them to be warm, affable, and lots of fun.

Vitals

rooms: 7, 4 with private baths, 3 share 2 full bathrooms

pets: no

pets in residence: none

smoking: not inside, but OK on porches or decks

open season: mostly year-round, closed for a few weeks either side of deep snow

rates: $60 through $90

rates include: breakfast

owners/innkeepers:
Dave and Terry Rose
6036 Barnhart Road
Ludington, MI 49431
(616) 843-8193

Windermere Inn .
Beulah

The Windermere Inn was built about 1895 and served as the homestead for a large working farm that wrapped around the northeast corner of Crystal Lake. It was surrounded by cherry orchards. You can still see the foundations of old outbuildings nearby, and there is an artesian well just out back. As the land changed ownership in this century, most of the acreage was sold off and began sprouting shops and houses. By 1980, the old farmhouse itself was vacant.

Bill and Loralee Ludwig passed by the house for years en route to their own residence on the north shore of Crystal Lake. They always admired the structure but felt it was too big for just the two of

them . . . until the day Loralee mentioned that it would make a nice bed-and-breakfast home.

They bought the structure in January, 1983, and spent four months repairing walls and ceilings, installing bathrooms, decorating, and filling it with country treasures. By the time they opened in July, they had brought warmth and sophistication back to the neglected lakeside home.

Guests stay in one of four upstairs sleeping rooms that echo the main floor's casual country style. Each room has a private bath and is accented with lovely curtains and bedcovers that were custom-made by Loralee and her daughter-in-law, Mary. Flowers, candy, and fruit greet each new arrival. If you are feeling sociable, you can join the innkeepers and the other guests in the living room or sitting room. Each has a fireplace that the Ludwigs keep fed on cold nights. Continental breakfast is served amid linen, silver, crystal, and fine china in the handsome dining room. Both Bill and Loralee smoke, and smoking is permitted throughout the home.

The Windermere Inn is a great place to hole up for a while with Crystal Lake just across the street and the quaint little villages of Beulah and Benzonia nearby to explore. But, it is also a good destination point from which to branch out during the day and return each evening. Within an easy drive are sandy Lake Michigan beaches, the Sleeping Bear Dunes National Lakeshore, Interlochen, numerous golf courses, small inland lakes with good fishing, and outstanding winter skiing.

Vitals

rooms: 4 with private baths

pets: no

pets in residence: none

smoking: yes

open season: April through February

rates: $65 per room that will accommodate two adults, two-night minimum in summer

rates include: Continental breakfast

owners/innkeepers:
    Bill and Loralee Ludwig
    747 Crystal Drive
    Beulah, MI 49617
    (616) 882-7264

A Country Place Bed and Breakfast, *South Haven*
Hidden Pond Farm, *Fennville*
The Inn at Union Pier, *Union Pier*
Kemah Guest House, *Saugatuck*
The Kirby House, *Saugatuck*
The Last Resort, *South Haven*
Old Holland Inn, *Holland*
The Park House, *Saugatuck*
Pebble House, *Lakeside*
The Porches, *Fennville*
The Ross, *South Haven*
Seascape Bed and Breakfast, *Grand Haven*
Stonegate Inn Bed and Breakfast, *Nunica*
Twin Gables Country Inn, *Saugatuck*
Wickwood Inn, *Saugatuck*
Woods and Hearth Bed and Breakfast, *Niles*
Yesterday's Inn Bed and Breakfast, *Niles*

The Southern Shore

A Country Place Bed and Breakfast
South Haven

We were sipping a glass of wine with Art and Lee Niffenegger on the back deck of their Country Place when Lee spotted a tiny, ruby-throated hummingbird. It was attracted to the abundance of flowers the inn-keepers had planted all around the home. Surrounded on three sides by woods, the yard is visited by scores of birds each day and even some small wildlife.

"We offer the best of both worlds here," Lee explained as we walked around the inn. And for those looking for a mix of country and city, it is true. The home sits on five and a half acres, just north of the South Haven city limits, yet is less than a five-minute drive from the city's shops, restaurants, and marina. Even better, it is right across the street from Lake Michigan and there is beach access for guests.

Art and Lee opened A Country Place in summer, 1986. Their inter-est in bed and breakfast was fostered when they lived in England for

two years. "We traveled to B & Bs every weekend," said Art, "and decided that was the way to go." They kept a list of the features they liked and included several of the ideas in their own inn. A few were adapted to the tastes and expectations of American travelers, such as the refrigerator you will find stocked with cold beverages for guests.

"In England, we were served hot tea in the afternoon," said Lee. "Americans have never picked up on that custom, so we offer our guests iced tea, soft drinks, or wine instead."

The original section of this home is a classic Greek Revival style built by Crosby Eaton in the early 1860s. Eaton raised fruit and grains and was active in politics. He served twelve terms as Caseo Township Supervisor, was superintendent of schools for six years, and served two terms as a representative in the state legislature.

The back section of the home was added in 1922, but it continues the Greek Revival theme so closely that it is difficult to tell the old and new sections apart. The country theme is carried out with small print wallpaper, baskets of dried flowers, wreaths, and antique furnishings. Quilts made by the Niffeneggers' daughter cover the beds, and ceiling fans cool the rooms in the summer. There is a wood-burning fireplace in the living room—a popular spot after an afternoon of cross-country skiing.

Breakfast in August was hot, homemade muffins and Lee's delicious, twelve-grain bread; a selection of cereals; big bowls of fresh peaches and blueberries; juice and coffee or tea. The air was brisk so we joined several guests at a handsome oak table on the summer porch. On warmer mornings, guests enjoy breakfast on the big, back deck. There is also a formal dining room with windows that look out onto the woods.

Ask Art and Lee about the new Kal-Haven Trail, which offers year-round outdoor activities, as well as the winery tours and pick-your-own fruit farms nearby. They can fill you in on all there is to see and do in the area.

Vitals

rooms: 4 most of the year, 5 in summer; 2 share 1 full bath, 2 have a private half bath and share a shower.

pets: no

pets in residence: 1 cat, not allowed in guest rooms

smoking: outside only

open season: year-round

rates: $45 through $55 double occupancy, singles Monday through Thursday $40

rates include: breakfast

owners/innkeepers:

Art and Lee Niffenegger
Route 5, Box 43
North Shore Drive
South Haven, MI 49090
(616) 637-5523

Hidden Pond Farm
Fennville

Ed Kennedy was in one of his gardens clipping daylilies when we arrived, and he appeared to be a man totally at peace with his surroundings. He greeted us warmly and gestured toward the flowers. "A friend told me, 'Plant and plan as though you're going to be here forever. You won't be, but someone else will be to enjoy what you've done.'" While showing us his home and recalling how Hidden Pond came to be, Ed mixed prose and poetry, some of his own and some of others, to present the total picture of what he offers guests. And it is this: a lovely home with fine traditional and antique furnishings; twenty-eight surrounding acres of meadow, ravine, and woods; and the opportunity to experience the beauty and peace of life at Hidden Pond Farm.

The first floor of the home is reserved for guests. There are two sleeping rooms, and with them comes use of the living room with a fireplace, a kitchen and dining room, a den, and a breakfast porch. Last summer, Ed added a deck that runs the length of the back of the home

overlooking the wooded grounds and installed doors so that both sleeping rooms have direct access to the deck. Like the side patio, it is furnished with elegant, black wrought-iron furniture.

Ed's own living quarters are in the lower level where he also prepares breakfast for his guests. He served it to us on the porch from which there was a fine view of the pond and of a lush cascade of morning glories. We enjoyed eggs and fresh melon and a rich, steaming, pecan sticky-bread, along with Ed's special coffee.

The pace here is relaxed. Guests are afforded a lot of privacy, yet the arrangement is especially nice for two couples traveling together.

Whether visitors choose to hole up in their rooms, take a walk, watch from the deck for deer that visit the pond, or take advantage of the area's many attractions, Ed hopes they will forget their cares and enjoy the pleasures of this quiet rural estate. He is part romantic, part counselor, part educator, retired from a busy career in the insurance

business. He has discovered a deep sense of peace at Hidden Pond Farm and thrives on sharing it.

Vitals

rooms: 2 with private baths

pets: no

pets in residence: none

smoking: yes

open season: year-round

rates: $75 per room for first night Sunday through Thursday, $90 per room Friday and Saturday, increased discounts for each additional weeknight and for renting both rooms

rates include: full breakfast

owner/innkeeper:
Edward X. Kennedy
P.O. Box 461
Fennville, MI 49408
(616) 561-2491

The Inn at Union Pier
Union Pier

There have been a lot of changes at the Inn at Union Pier since we first saw it two years ago.

"All the rooms are completed now," Bill told us as we walked through the expansive Great Room and into the new glassed-in dining room. From there we could see the other two buildings joined by a porch and wooden walkway, that make up this handsome compound. It is set amid sixty-foot-tall oaks and Madeleine's perennial flower gardens. A flagstone courtyard hosts a variety of birds and doubles as a summer dining area.

The Great Room serves as a gathering area for all the guests. It is appointed with groupings of furniture upholstered in prints of pink, plum, and forest green that echo colors in the area rugs. Sheer lace panels drape six sets of windows. During one of our visits, a guest was practicing Schubert on the grand piano. The room is heated by a massive Swedish Kakelugn tiled, wood-burning stove. It has five interior

chimneys that process the smoke and gently heat the air while keeping the exterior tile comfortably warm to the touch.

The inns sleeping rooms are furnished with antiques and elegant reproductions, and several have Kakelugn stoves in different styles. A few are quite old, including a round stove built in 1930 that has delicate dandelion designs on the tiles. The Terrace Suite, with its queen-sized cherry sleigh bed and wet bar, has a private balcony that we found to be a delightful spot for reading the morning paper.

Breakfast includes butter-melting popovers and fresh fruit with a rum-flavored blend of sweet cream, sour cream, and nutmeg. Guests might also find steaming French toast or a rich quiche. There is an outdoor hot tub to relax in, and for swimming, it is hard to beat Lake Michigan just across the street. Bill says the area also offers great cross-country skiing, and he installed a rack to hold guests' skis.

In the few years that Madeleine and Bill have owned the Inn at Union Pier, it has caught the eye of newspaper and magazine editors across the country and gained a national reputation for hospitality excellence. It is indeed a memorable, genteel inn with a winning combination of good food, great location, appealing decor, and two fine innkeepers.

Vitals

rooms: 15 with private baths

pets: no

pets in residence: 1 cat, seldom seen, and 1 dog, confined to the first floor

smoking: yes

open season: year-round

rates: $85 through $110 double occupancy, 2-night minimum on weekends, 3-night minimum on holidays

rates include: breakfast

owners/innkeepers:

Bill and Madeleine Reinke

P.O. Box 222

9708 Berrien

Union Pier, MI 49129

(616) 469-4700

Kemah Guest House
Saugatuck

Kemah is an Indian word that loosely translates as "in the teeth of the wind," and that is where you will find this hilltop home. The oldest part of the structure is believed to have been built in 1906. William J. Springer, an old-world German who sat on the Chicago Board of Trade, bought the estate in 1926 and added unusual Art Deco touches such as a half-circle solarium with leaded glass windows and corner lights, and a tiled fireplace in the living room. Art Deco is often characterized by the predominant use of black and gold with pastel accents. It is very striking but infrequently seen because of the relatively short duration of its

popularity. Springer also commissioned artist Carl Hoerman, a wood-carver, to produce ornate beams, carved panel landscapes, and cornice boards that can be seen throughout the home. He carved Springer's coat of arms in one panel, and in another, this poem:

> In rain and shine
> my port divine
> a world my own
> Kemah my home

There are more surprises. A path that leads to the back of the house will take you to a small cave, complete with stalactites and stalagmites, that Springer built. If you walk along the side property, you will find a stone with poetic verse that marks the grave of an Indian.

Terry and Cindi Tatsch bought Kemah in 1982 and opened for bed-and-breakfast guests in 1984. "We wanted to restore the home with respect to the integrity of its historic architecture," Terry explained. They decorated the large second-floor sleeping rooms with matched late-Victorian furniture sets and beautiful linens that suggest the comfortable life-style Springer must have enjoyed. All the rooms are sizable. Suite Enchantment, the largest, also has a lovely adjacent sitting room

that makes it a perfect selection if you plan to stay in the area for a few days, or if you are bringing a briefcase of paperwork. In 1988, the home was added to the State Register of Historic Places.

The Continental breakfast is set on silver trays and guests are welcome to eat wherever they want. We chose the bright sun room furnished in wicker with imported Dutch lace curtains and enjoyed the company of other guests staying at this fine hilltop guesthouse.

Vitals

rooms: 6 that share 3 full baths

pets: no

pets in residence: 1 dog, not allowed in guest quarters

smoking: outside only

open season: year-round

rates: $75 through $95 double occupancy, weekday and senior citizen discounts, 2-night minimum on weekends May through September

rates include: breakfast

owners/innkeepers:
Terry and Cindi Tatsch
633 Pleasant
Saugatuck, MI 49453
(616) 857-2919

The Kirby House
Saugatuck

The Kirby House is a familiar landmark to many in the Saugatuck-Douglas area. It was built just prior to 1890 by Sara Kirby; when she left in 1932, her daughter, who was a nurse, turned the home into a hospital. Over several years it grew from three beds to nineteen and played an important role in the lives of hundreds of area residents until it closed in the late 1950s.

Loren and Marsha Kontio had enjoyed staying in bed-and-breakfast homes throughout Europe and the United States, and they wanted to open their own. By the time they looked at the Kirby House in 1983, it had gone through several ownership and use changes and needed a lot of work. But the Kontios also saw that it had strong pluses—beautiful woodwork, striking architecture, and a site already zoned for commercial use. Their friends rallied around them enthusiastically and offered to help with the renovation. The Kontios purchased it the following

December and began working on it in January. As promised, their friends showed up en masse to help. "Sometimes we had twenty people here on a work weekend," Marsha explained. In all, they estimate that more than forty people helped put the inn together, and the work was completed in just sixteen weekends. They opened in time for the Holland Tulip Festival.

To complement the Victorian architecture, Marsha and Loren selected small print wallpaper and period furnishings, including many oak and brass pieces. The handsome dining room, paneled in the original quarter-sawn oak, becomes an additional sleeping room in the summer. For the added pleasure of their guests, they installed a large outdoor deck, a swimming pool, and a hot tub. A buffet breakfast that includes fresh fruit and juices, croissants and muffins, and coffees and teas is offered each morning. In the winter, the four fireplaces are stoked for cozy comfort, and guests may cross-country ski at the nearby

golf course. Warm beverages simmering on the wood-burning stove await their return.

Marsha and Loren have one house rule, that people make themselves at home and treat Kirby House like their own. They try to spend some time with each guest, to get to know them and make them feel welcome. The Kontios are gracious innkeepers and have brought new life to this fine old home.

Vitals

rooms: 8 in winter, 10 in summer; 4 have private baths, 2 have private baths not attached, and 4 share 2 baths

pets: ask the innkeeper

pets in residence: 1 cat and 1 dog, seldom seen

smoking: yes

open season: year round

rates: $75 through $85 per room weekends, $65 through $75 per room Sunday through Thursday, $10 per extra person in same room

rates include: breakfast buffet

owners/innkeepers: Marsha and Loren Kontio

manager:

David Manke
Center Street at Blue Star Highway
P.O. Box 1174
Saugatuck, MI 49453
(616) 857-2904

The Last Resort
South Haven

Sunsets are magnificent over Lake Michigan, and the large front deck at the Last Resort is a great place from which to observe them and the rest of the goings-on in this busy harbor town. The inn's beautifully painted and trimmed siding, the neat walk and tended grounds give no hint of the condition it was in when Wayne and Mary Babcock bought it less than half a dozen years ago.

Constructed in 1883 by Civil War Captain Barney Dyckman, the building was actually, according to the Babcocks' research, South Haven's first resort. But its spectacular location and once-glorious past could not save it from the fate that struck so many great old summer inns around the middle of this century. By the time Wayne and Mary bought it in 1979, it had been vacant for twenty-five years and was

suffering from neglect. They spent three years renovating—installing a new roof, leveling floors, plastering, painting, and decorating, to produce the comfortable lakeside bed-and-breakfast inn you will find today.

Fourteen pretty sleeping rooms occupy two levels of the expansive second floor. Each room is individually decorated with a colorful combination of printed wallpaper, comforters, and handloomed rugs. Each also has a skirted corner sink with hot and cold water and a handsome wooden shaving cabinet. To combat the mid-summer heat, air-conditioning was recently added.

Characteristic of many lakeside inns, the rooms are small to medium in size and a few have additional sleeping or sitting areas. Adjoining rooms may be rented as suites. Guests have easy access to the beach, just across the street, and to the shops and towns up and down the

shore. The Last Resort's breakfast room doubles as a lounge in the afternoons and evenings, and it was the scene of some hot games of euchre when we visited.

Both Mary and Wayne are also artists. Mary's monotypes and Wayne's bronze jewelry are on display and for sale at the inn gallery, where guests register.

While still in the grip of "rehab fever," the Babcocks purchased a small guesthouse next door and have renovated it, also. It has two levels, two full baths, and will accommodate eight to ten people. A newly completed "Doll House" cottage adjacent to the inn will sleep two and is available by the week. Ask for details.

Vitals

rooms: 14, 8 have connecting doors and may be rented individually or as 2-room suites, all rooms share several common bathrooms with separate facilities for men and women

pets: no

pets in residence: none

smoking: there are smoking and nonsmoking areas

open season: late April to September 1; September and October, weekends only

rates: $42 through $62 double occupancy, suites $94, $4 less for single occupancy, 5 nights for the price of 4

rates include: Continental breakfast

owners/innkeepers:
Wayne and Mary Babcock
86 North Shore Drive
South Haven, MI 49090
(616) 637-8943

Old Holland Inn
Holland

Dave and Fran Plaggemars' handsome bed-and-breakfast home sits on a quiet, tree-lined cul-de-sac in the heart of a historic district. It is a fine, old neighborhood, comprised of four square blocks of residences all listed on the national register of historic homes. At the end of the street is the city's oldest elementary school.

John J. Cappon was secretary of his family's Cappon-Bertsch Leather Company when he had this home built in 1895. His father, Issac, was a wealthy industrialist and Holland's first mayor. Dave and Fran bought the house in November, 1985, and were sixteenth in a sequence of owners that included town industrialists and Hope College presidents.

"We had stayed in a lot of bed-and-breakfast homes," Dave explained. "We liked them, they were our style of traveling and we found it stimulating. Bed and breakfast also seemed like a good business opportunity, and when we found this house, the timing was right." The Plaggemars began renovation immediately and opened for bed-and-breakfast guests the following spring.

Fran is relatively new to the Holland area. She was raised in Phila-
delphia and is now a student of art at nearby Hope College. Dave, on the
other hand, is a native of Holland whose kin were among the city's ten
original families. He is a social worker with experience in juvenile
crime, and drug and substance abuse. His current focus is on corporate
consultation for employee-related problems.

The Plaggemars' guests have their choice of four second-floor
sleeping rooms. Three are large and furnished with antique bedsteads
including one that Dave and Fran found in the attic of this home. Our
room had an ornately carved walnut bed and a tall walnut dresser, both
with striking burl veneer. Dotted Swiss curtains were draped with a rich
burgundy swag. As with the other guest rooms, ours had antique accessories, a smooth-working transom, and turn-of-the century touches

such as a doily-draped table and brass blanket stand. The fourth room is the former maid's chamber. It is smaller and cozy with twin beds and lace curtains.

While stained-glass windows and oak woodwork add elegance to the spacious first floor, the focal point is the living room fireplace with its original, ornate, brass insert and hand-carved oak mantle. It is a favorite gathering place for guests in the winter after returning from cross-country skiing or a walk by the lake. The artwork throughout the house is a combination of Fran's own work and that of some of her accomplished peers.

Although their careers keep them busy, Fran and Dave take the time to prepare a plentiful, sit-down breakfast for their guests. A colorful fruit plate and a cheese plate are served along with a variety of home-baked muffins or breads and pastries from the Dutch bakery just down the street. The dining room table is set with linens and china, some of which were passed to Fran from her grandmother who ran a boardinghouse in Philly. When the weather is good, guests enjoy breakfast on the back deck.

If you are partial, as we are, to Dutch sweets, have Dave and Fran point you in the direction of the bakery so you can stock up on almond-filled Banket and windmill cookies before you leave town.

Vitals

rooms: 4, 1 with a private bath, 3 that share 1 bath
pets: no
pets in residence: 2 cats
smoking: no
open season: year-round
rates: $45 through $75 double occupancy
rates include: breakfast
owners/innkeepers:
    David and Fran Plaggemars
    133 West 11th Street
    Holland, MI 49423
    (616) 396-6601

The Park House
Saugatuck

Lumberman Horace D. Moore originally owned much of the land on the east side of the Kalamazoo River in Saugatuck. He operated a shingle mill and a sawmill there, and ran two ships to transport the wood to Chicago. Moore built a large home on Holland Street in 1857, fenced a parklike parcel of land around it, and kept a herd of deer to delight his children. The townspeople nicknamed his estate the Park House—a designation that has lasted 130 years.

Susan B. Anthony came to the Park House at the request of Mrs. Moore, who was concerned about the lack of temperance in the town. Anthony helped found the local chapter of the Women's Christian Temperance Union (WCTU) and was successful in closing six of the town's fourteen saloons during her visit.

By early 1984, the Park House was showing signs of age and neglect. But Joe and Lynda Petty saw its potential. They purchased the

house in January of that year and opened for guests six months later after a whirlwind restoration that included complete cosmetic work plus the addition of central heat, eight bathrooms, a new electrical system, and a new porch. The decor is country, from the brass beds and printed wallpaper to the bowl and pitcher sets, crocks of flowers, ruffled curtains, and rag rugs. We admired the recent acquisition of photos of the Moore family and a framed piece of lace that was given to Winnie Moore, the eldest Moore daughter, on her wedding day in 1887. The sleeping rooms are small and bright. They have been named after members of the Moore family, and you will find items in each that reflect the namesake. Mrs. Moore's room, for example, has a collection of spools and thread, as though she were about to sit down to her

mending. Rooms named for the daughters hold a few toys and other children's things. It is quite a nice touch.

In 1987, the Pettys added a wing for their own living quarters and a cool, north-facing screened porch for guests that overlooks a lush garden area. They also opened a two-bedroom suite on the third floor and air-conditioned the entire inn.

Breakfast is served in the big country dining room. It includes a variety of muffins, granola, fresh fruit, and juice. Lynda said she encourages people to linger at the table and talk. She keeps check-in and checkout times flexible so that guests will not feel rushed. Adjacent to the dining room is a comfortable sitting room with a TV and fireplace. Fishermen will find the inn's proximity to the Kalamazoo River and Lake Michigan especially convenient. Lynda and Joe have arrangements with several charter boats and will put together special packages that include an early breakfast and a sendoff with a thermos of tea or coffee and a picnic lunch.

Vitals

rooms: 9 rooms with private baths

pets: no

pets in residence: 1 cat and 1 dog

smoking: not in the sleeping rooms, but permitted in designated common areas

open season: year-round

rates: $65 through $80 double occupancy, $120 for suite that accommodates 4, additional persons are $15

rates include: breakfast

owners/innkeepers:
Joe and Lynda Petty
888 Holland
Saugatuck, MI 49453
(616) 857-4535

Pebble House
Lakeside

The Pebble House with its jaunty stone facade is instantly recognizable while driving south from tiny Lakeside on Lake Shore Road. It was built as a summer home in 1910 by two couples who were retired from working in the circus. Later, a rapid succession of owners and uses left the estate suffering from neglect. Ed and Jean Lawrence bought the home in August, 1983. It was dilapidated, but had unquestionable character and some surviving attributes. Among them are a late-Victorian-style etched window, a stone fireplace, and wide glassed-in porches. As an artist, Jean approached the project like a giant painting, and the transformation is remarkable.

The main house, with four sleeping rooms and several common rooms, has been completely renovated along with the "little house" and two-story coach house that border the Pebble House tennis court. All the rooms are outfitted with handsome oak and walnut furniture that dates from the turn of the century through the early 1930s. Many of the pieces are massive, comfortable Mission styles that invite curling up

with a book, or settling in for late-night conversations. The Lilac Suite in the coach house will accommodate two couples. The Raspberry Suite in the "little house" has a wood-burning stove and kitchenette and may be rented with the adjoining Blueberry Suite to accommodate six. Guests often end the day sitting by the fireplace talking with others or playing cards together. But several common areas and cozy· corners provide ample room for those seeking quiet moments alone. During the summer of 1986, Ed and Jean added a large screen house that is perfect for enjoying the glorious breezes coming off Lake Michigan, just across the street. Nearby, you will find areas for canoeing, hiking, bird-watching, bicycling, and cross-country skiing. The well-known Warren Dunes are only about ten minutes away.

Ed works in Chicago during the week and comes to Lakeside on the weekends. Because he is city oriented, he acts as a catalyst for different directions of conversation. He and Jean have traveled extensively and have fascinating stories of their experiences, not the least of which is their wedding that took place in a seaman's chapel in Malmo, Sweden. Their love of Scandinavian traditions inspired their selection of break-

fast items that include a cold buffet with cheeses, sausages, herring, pastry, and fruit. We loved it! It is served family style around a big dining room table where guests often linger and talk until noon.

The inn is open year-round, subject to the roads being clear in the winter. If you want to reach the area by train, Amtrak stops in New Buffalo and you can make arrangements for Jean and Ed to pick you up. You can also be picked up in Michigan City, Indiana, if you ride the South Shore out of Chicago with Ed.

Vitals

rooms: 3 guest buildings house 7 rooms with private baths, 3 are
    2-room suites, 1 guest apartment is available by the week

pets: no

pets in residence: 4 cats, restricted to common rooms

smoking: discouraged

open season: year-round

rates: $80 through $90 double occupancy

rates include: Scandinavian cold buffet breakfast; 1 suite has
    kitchenette

owners/innkeepers:
    Jean and Ed Lawrence
    15093 Lake Shore Road
    Lakeside, MI 49116
    (616) 469-1416

The Porches
Fennville

"The lake hit 80 degrees this summer," Bob Johnson told us when we visited last August. We were standing on the porch of his ninety-year-old summer home admiring the view of Lake Michigan just across the street. This area, located three miles south of Saugatuck, is called Pier Cove and was a busy lumber town in the mid-1800s. The home has been in Bob's family since it was built in 1897. It earned its name from the covered porches that wrap entirely around both the first and second floor. Last year the Porches was added to the State Register of Historic Places.

Bob and his wife opened the home for bed-and-breakfast guests in 1987. "I was too young to retire," Bob explained, "and we were looking for an additional source of income. We watched B & Bs flourish in Saugatuck and thought this homestead would adapt well."

The five sleeping rooms—one on the first floor and four on the second—open directly onto the porches rather than to an inside stair or hall. That is the original design, and each sleeping room is a corner room with two sets of windows to take advantage of the good lake breezes.

In the front of the house, on the first floor, is a large common room with a table for playing cards and games, a TV, and shelves full of books in case you forget to bring one. Bob builds a fire in the fireplace on chilly days.

The home is furnished in a casual cottage style. Each sleeping room has twin reading lamps over the bed and a ceiling fan, an antique dresser or desk, and a sitting area with chairs and a small table. The rooms are carpeted and spotlessly clean. Many of the home's turn-of-the-century family visitors were schoolteachers who came for the whole summer. To accommodate their trunks and traveling gear, the sleeping rooms had large, deep closets that Bob and Ellen converted to full bathrooms.

The Johnson's living quarters are in the annex attached to the inn and breakfast is served in their dining room between 8:30 and 11:00. Guests will find fresh fruit in season, assorted sweet rolls and muffins, a choice of cereals, juice, and beverages.

When people come to this side of the state they visit the vineyards, the antique shops, and fruit farms, but mostly, says Bob, they come because of the lake. And when they stay at the Porches, they can enjoy 200 feet of private Lake Michigan beach. The home itself sits on about an acre and a quarter of land that is wooded and peaceful. "Our guests have a tendency to sleep in," Bob observed. "I think it's the combination of fresh air and good beds!"

Vitals

rooms: 5 rooms with private bath

pets: no

pets in residence: none

smoking: not in the house, but OK on covered porches

open season: May 1 through November 1

rates: $49 through $59 double occupancy

rates include: breakfast

owners/innkeepers:
Bob and Ellen Johnson
2297 Lakeshore Drive
Fennville, MI 49408
(616) 543-4162

Kingsley H. 561-6425

Crane H. 561-6931

Hutchins Mar 543-4384

Fenn Inn 561-2836

The Ross
South Haven

When Cathy Hormann and Brad Wilcox settled on the idea of opening a bed and breakfast home, they began a search from St. Joseph to Kalamazoo for the perfect residence. They found their dream house in South Haven: a 102-year-old Queen Anne built by lumber tycoon Volney Ross and owned by members of the Ross family for 91 years. Its last family resident was Volney's son Arthur, an eccentric millionaire who made his fortune in the stock market.

After Arthur Volney died in 1975, the home went through a succession of owners until Brad and Cathy bought it in 1985. They worked nights and weekends, often until midnight, refurbishing the old home and completing four sleeping rooms in time to open for business the following summer. By 1987, they had finished three more sleeping rooms and added a full bath.

The house is located in a quiet residential neighborhood just a few blocks from downtown. "We're close to everything," explained Cathy.

"Guests can walk to the restaurants and shops in town, and we're just three blocks from Lake Michigan."

The sleeping rooms offer variety in decor and amenities. A large first-floor room and private half bath are conveniently located just off the living room. Two of the second-floor rooms have pretty Laura Ashley wall coverings with matching linens. One room has a double bed plus a trundle bed that opens to a double bed. Another has a double, white, four-poster bed and a white wicker daybed—perfect for guests traveling with an older child. The smallest sleeping room, that which Arthur chose as his own, has a water bed. There are ceiling fans in all the rooms and handmade guest robes in the closets. Here and there you'll find a grapevine or dried flower wreath and other country accents.

The big living room has a TV and VCR. Cathy and Brad rent movies on the weekends for guests who, they have observed, are sometimes so tired from their day's activities that they enjoy being able to sit back and

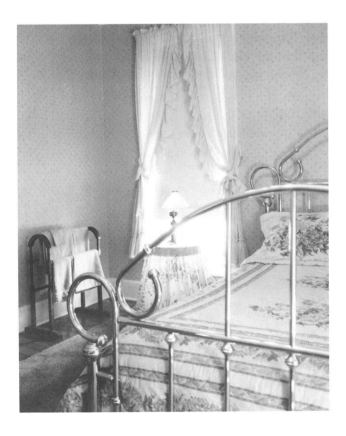

watch a show. There is a hot tub, too, which doubled as a cool pool during the heat of 1988.

Cathy works as a paralegal in Kalamazoo and Brad is an engineer for Zenith in St. Joseph, so breakfast is usually rolls and coffee during the week, with Cathy's daughter, Judie, assisting. But weekend guests are in for a treat. "This morning, for example, we served crab souffle and blueberry buckle," Cathy delighted in telling us one warm Sunday afternoon in August. "Guests love it in the summer on Sunday mornings when they can sit out here on the porch and listen to the bells and the choir in the neighborhood church."

The innkeepers are members of Friends of the Kal-Haven Trail and can tell you all about the facility. They will also recommend good routes around the town for bicycle riding so you can see some of South Haven's other historic turn-of-the century homes.

Vitals

rooms: 7, they share 3 full baths, 1 has a private half bath

pets: no

pets in residence: none

smoking: not inside, but OK on covered porches

open season: year-round

rates: $40 through $55 double occupancy, $10 per extra person in the same room

rates include: Continental breakfast Monday through Friday, full breakfast Saturday and Sunday

owners/innkeepers:

Cathy Hormann and Brad Wilcox
229 Michigan
South Haven, MI 49090
(616) 637-2256

Seascape Bed and Breakfast
Grand Haven

Norm and Susan Meyer's ranch-style house is nestled on a dune on the beach, a few doors from the Grand Haven harbor. It is a straight shot from their deck to the cooling waters of Lake Michigan, as we discovered one summer when both the air and the lake were setting record high temperatures.

The Meyers moved here in 1979. A few years later, they stayed at a bed-and-breakfast home in Shipshewana, Indiana, "and just fell in love with the concept," remembers Susan.

They knew their lakeside home with its prime beach location had a lot to offer travelers, and they were coming to a crossroad in their lives when they could set off in new directions. "The children were growing up and leaving home," said Susan. "The timing was perfect." They opened for bed-and-breakfast lodging in summer 1986.

The first thing you will notice at Seascape is the view that, from nearly every room in the house, is spectacular. Windows across the first-floor gathering room offer a 180-degree panorama of the blue shoreline and the harbor to the south. There are two sleeping rooms on the first floor, including the Lakeview room that has a small sitting area by the windows. For guests wanting a little more room or privacy, there is the Harborside suite on the lower level with a master bedroom, an optional smaller sleeping room, a private bath, and a big sitting room. Sliding glass doors open onto a patio and the path to the beach. This is a good setup for couples traveling together or for adults with a child. The second sleeping room is reserved for occupants of the suite.

Furnishings vary from country to contemporary. There is a great fieldstone fireplace in the gathering room bedecked with decoys, fishing memorabilia, and nautical items. Baskets and dried flowers hang from wooden beams. In the Ashley room, you will find a stately, antique bed with a six-foot-tall carved oak headboard, while in the Lakeview room, guests are treated to a night on a queen-sized flotation water bed. The Harborside, which frequently hosts honeymoon or anniversary couples, has a romantic four-poster bed.

Susan pulls the rope on an old ringside bell to call guests for breakfast. We feasted on a rich egg casserole with sausage and cheese, muffins, croissants, and a selection of fruits and juices. On other days, the menu might include pancakes or French toast. When the weather is good, breakfast is served on the wide deck that overlooks the lake. Guests have been known to stretch out on the lounges there in the late evening and fall asleep watching the stars.

While summer seems to be the most popular season for beach going, do not overlook the colder months of the year when the lake and surrounding woodlands offer a dramatic change in scenery.

"Some of the most beautiful times of the year occur when storms are coming across the lake or when the ice is forming," said Norm. "In spring and fall we can watch the migration of birds, and in winter the lake looks like a mountain range of ice."

In addition to being an avid fisherman, Norm is a former pilot and police officer. Susan is a nurse. Both are warm, engaging people who make their guests feel welcome and very much at home. They offer a choice of beverages on arrival, which always seems to break the ice for guests who are new to bed-and-breakfast travel. To help their guests enjoy Grand Haven, they keep copies of local restaurant menus and can lend seasoned advice about tourist spots in the area.

Vitals

rooms: 2 first-floor rooms with private baths, and the Harborside suite that has a private bath

pets: no

pets in residence: no

smoking: not in the sleeping rooms

open season: year-round

rates: $65 through $75 double occupancy

rates include: breakfast

owners/innkeepers:
Susan and Norm Meyer
20009 Breton
Spring Lake, MI 49456
(616) 842-8409

note: Seascape is within the city limits of Grand Haven but has a Spring Lake mailing address.

Stonegate Inn Bed and Breakfast
Nunica

The Stonegate Inn is located just about midway between Muskegon and Grand Rapids, and for a time in its 128-year history, it was known to travelers as the halfway house along that route. It was also the Ernst family home for 100 years. Present owners are John and Cleo Ludwick. They purchased the inn in May, 1985, from the Zartman family who had opened for bed-and-breakfast lodging the previous summer. The Ludwicks have filled it with family antiques and fine Early-American reproductions by Carl Forslund, a well-known Grand Rapids furniture manufacturer.

Guests share a common room with a TV and games on the second floor. Continental breakfast is served in the formal dining room or, by request, in a guest's room. This stately brick structure has been beautifully maintained and is visible from I-96.

Vitals

rooms: 4 sleeping rooms, including 1 single; 1 with private bath, 3 that share 1 bath

pets: no

pets in residence: 1 barn cat

smoking: outside only

open season: year-round

rates: $35 single room, $60 through $75 double

rates include: Continental breakfast

owners/innkeepers:
John and Cleo Ludwick
10831 Cleveland
Nunica, MI 49448
(616) 837-9267

Twin Gables Country Inn
Saugatuck

Denise and Mike Simcik discovered Saugatuck by accident. They used to boat around Wisconsin's Door County Peninsula and decided one year to head inland by river to St. Louis. On the first day of their trip, they were advised of the hazards of river navigation and decided to follow the Lake Michigan shore instead. They came into Saugatuck on a Friday, fully intending to leave in a couple of days, but bad weather held them until the following Tuesday. It gave them time to take a stroll around the town, and they fell in love with it. Two weeks later, they returned to take a serious look at what was available to develop as a business. Their choice was a small hotel, formerly called Twin Gables, located just across the street from the Kalamazoo River.

According to the tax rolls, Twin Gables was built in 1865 at the river's edge and used as a boardinghouse for employees of the nearby stave mill. When the lumber industry began to decline in the twenties, it was converted to a hotel. In 1936, the Blue Star highway was built and Twin Gables was moved from the river to its present location. After lean

years during the Depression, the hotel made a temporary comeback. Townspeople have told the Simciks that they remember the hotel's excellent cuisine during that time and that it was the scene of many social events. But it closed again in the late fifties and remained so until Denise and Mike purchased it in 1982.

The hotel originally had sixteen small second-floor sleeping rooms that shared two baths. Mike and Denise redesigned the space and added a wing to produce eleven good-sized sleeping rooms on the second floor, each with a private bath and sitting area, plus three large sleeping rooms on the first floor. One is a suite with a living room alcove and sofa sleeper. All are decorated differently, and each has a name that aptly describes its furnishings, such as the Jenny Lind Room, the Shangri-La Room, and the Tartan Room. Denise painted stencils and hand cut wallpaper borders to carry out the individual themes. Her decorating talents are matched by her fluency in languages. In addition to English, Denise speaks French, Maltese, and Italian.

A living room and dining room share the expansive, open first floor and are decorated with country furnishings. Original decorative embossed tin covers the walls and ceiling. Float glass windows across the front give guests a view of the river. Several choices of breads and

baked goods, along with fruit and juice, are offered for breakfast each morning. Guests are welcome to eat in the dining room or on the enclosed veranda that spans the front of the inn. A large side lawn is available for picnics and summer games.

New to the inn in the last couple of years are a heated swimming pool and an indoor Jacuzzi, which is an especially welcome sight after a day of cross-country skiing. Air-conditioning is available.

Vitals

rooms: 14 with private baths

pets: no

pets in residence: 2 dogs restricted to common rooms

smoking: on first floor, preferred, discouraged in sleeping rooms

open season: year-round

rates: $34 through $89 double occupancy, which includes discounts for off-season

rates include: Continental breakfast

owners/innkeepers:
Denise and Mike Simcik
900 Lake Street
P.O. Box 881
Saugatuck, MI 49453
(616) 857-4346

Wickwood Inn
Saugatuck

If you walk north on Butler Street past Saugatuck's fine shops and galleries, you will come upon the lovely Wickwood Inn. Saugatuck residents Sue and Stub Louis had hoped for years that someone would open an inn in the picturesque village. After a memorable visit to the Duke's Hotel in London, and with two successful Saugatuck businesses already under their belts, they decided to try it themselves.

The solid 1930s apartment house purchased for the purpose was originally built by the family of Frank Wicks, one of Saugatuck's mayors. Prior to that, there was a dwelling on the site belonging to William

Butler, the village's first white settler and the man for whom the main street is named.

Sue wanted to create an inn that would be a wonderful surprise. She wanted it to be the finest escape, but still practical, warm, and above all, comfortable. To carry out the plan, she went to work on the interior with miles of fabrics and wall coverings by British designer Laura Ashley. Each of the eleven sleeping rooms is decorated around a different theme. The resulting effects are sometimes rich and handsome, sometimes sweet and dreamy, and they are all splendid. Four of the rooms represent the seasons of the year. Another four are suites with sitting areas. The largest suite has a huge four-poster bed and a fireplace flanked by a full wall of honey colored cedar. All of its furnishings are from the Baker Historic Charleston collection.

In each room, guests will find special touches: cozy down comforters, a hardwood armoire or a marble-topped writing desk, a hand-crocheted canopy, white wicker, fruit baskets, and original paintings. Each also has a private bath with soaps and shampoos by Crabtree and Evelyn.

A cozy, dark, mahogany library bar on the first floor is stocked with setups and good books. Beyond it is the sunken garden room with casual, cushioned wicker furniture and game tables. A set of French doors lead to a screened gazebo that takes advantage of the summer breezes coming off nearby Lake Michigan. During cooler months, guests enjoy gathering by the fireplace in the formal living room.

There is a lot to see here, such as Stub's collection of trains, antique trucks, and cars in the toy room. There are wooden shutters, beautiful rugs, and family heirlooms as well. Everything fits beautifully into the grand scheme.

Wickwood's staff is noticeably accommodating without being obtrusive, and we have always felt well cared for here. We recommend Wickwood to anyone wanting to add to their book of good memories. It is a delightful inn.

Vitals

rooms: 11 with private baths

pets: no

pets in residence: none

smoking: yes

open season: year-round

rates: $75 through $110, discounts during nonpeak seasons and to groups renting the entire inn; inquire about business packages

rates include: Continental breakfast, hors d'oeuvres, and setups at teatime

owners/innkeepers:
Sue and Stub Louis
510 Butler Street
Saugatuck, MI 49453
(616) 857-1097

Woods and Hearth Bed and Breakfast
Niles

Niles is a hilly, riverside city with a busy downtown and a big antique mall. It's close to Fernwood Nature Center, Tabor Hill Winery, miles of good cross-country ski trails, numerous restaurants, and Lake Michigan's Warren Dunes. Just over the state line in Indiana are Notre Dame and the Shipshewana Flea Market. This is not a big tourist area, in fact, it is a part of the state that a lot of people have never seen, but it has much to offer, including warm hospitality at Woods and Hearth Bed and Breakfast.

Nan Behre and A. J. Myers bought this impressive colonial brick home in November, 1985, and opened for travelers the following summer. Their guests have access to urban amenities along with the peace and quiet of the country, as Woods and Hearth sits on nine acres of woods, lawn, and garden just a mile from the center of town. To enhance the natural setting, Nan and A. J. maintain walking trails, as well as several feeders that draw birds and small animals to the yard. From the first-floor sun room, you can watch all the backyard activities.

Both Nan and A. J. have traveled extensively and lived overseas, Nan in Belgium and England, A. J. in Italy and Asia, including seven years as a prisoner of war. They both speak French—Nan is fluent—and A. J. can find his way through Italian. All this is background to give you an idea of their furnishings—numerous fascinating pieces, acquired in their travels, such as intricate inlaid wooden chairs and oriental art.

The five second-floor sleeping rooms are tastefully furnished with more traditional decor. They are bright and airy and large enough to settle into for a few days while you explore the area. Breakfast here is delicious. We were served fresh fruit, blueberry muffins, and a rich, delicate quiche. While Nan varies the menu, it is clear that there is always plenty of food. When the house is full of guests, breakfast is served buffet-style in the dining room. If Nan's son Chris stops in during your visit, ask him to play you a few tunes. Chris is a musician living in Chicago and he writes wonderful songs. We were treated to an impromptu concert on the back lawn one sunny Sunday morning.

There are many ways to get to Niles, not the least of which is via Amtrak, which makes several stops daily at the recently renovated depot. With advance notice, Nan and A. J. will be happy to pick you up.

Vitals

rooms: 5, 2 have private baths, 3 share 1 bath

pets: no

pets in residence: 1 small dog

smoking: not in the sleeping rooms

open season: year-round

rates: $37 through $49

rates include: breakfast

owners/innkeepers:

    Nan Behre and A. J. Myers

    950 South Third Street

    Niles, MI 49120

    (616) 683-0876

Yesterday's Inn Bed and Breakfast
Niles

Dawn and Phil Semler's beautiful brick bed-and-breakfast home was built in 1875. They purchased it in 1980 and filled it with lovely antiques as well as furniture, art, and rugs that reflect their travels to England and Korea, where they were stationed for several years when Phil was with the Air Force. Turn-of-the-century antiques mix graciously with brass-detailed Korean chests, oriental glass tables, brass rubbings, and Dawn's own paintings.

Three pretty antique-filled and air-conditioned sleeping rooms on the first and second floors are available to overnight guests. The exceptionally large Great Room in the basement is furnished with a king-sized bed, a full-sized sleeper sofa, a kitchen, a TV, and a full bath. It may be rented overnight or on a short-term basis as an apartment. Guests are welcome to share the spacious first-floor living room, patio, and hot tub. An elegant breakfast that usually includes muffins, quiche, potatoes, fruit juice, and a choice of cereal is served in the formal dining room. The menu is varied for guests staying more than one night.

There are many year-round activities that attract people to the area. Dawn says the cross-country skiing is great. Niles gets good, deep snow-falls and there are snowmobile trails maintained in fields leased by the state. Ski World is located in nearby Buchanan. Berrien Springs, fifteen miles away, has a fish ladder that makes salmon fishing popular around the area. I first discovered Yesterday's Inn while on business in South Bend, Indiana, just eight miles south. I can attest to its convenient location and the hospitality of Dawn and Phil. And while I cannot guarantee that there will be hot, homemade peanut butter cookies when you get there (my timing was perfect), I know you will get the kind of personal attention that makes staying in a bed-and-breakfast home so special.

Vitals

rooms: 4 with private baths

pets: no

pets in residence: 1 cat, not allowed in guest rooms

smoking: not in the house

open season: year-round

rates: $45 single or double occupancy, $5 children under 12 in same room with parents, $10 children over 12 in same room with parents

rates include: full breakfast

owners/innkeepers:

Dawn and Phil Semler
518 North 4th
Niles, MI 49120
(616) 683-6079

Briaroaks Inn, *Adrian*
Chicago Street Inn, *Brooklyn*
Clifford Lake Hotel, *Stanton*
Hall House Bed and Breakfast, *Kalamazoo*
McCarthy's Bear Creek Inn, *Marshall*
The Mendon Country Inn, *Mendon*
Mulberry House, *Owosso*
Munro House Bed and Breakfast, *Jonesville*
National House Inn, *Marshall*
The Old Lamp-Lighter's Homestay, *Battle Creek*
River Haven, *White Pigeon*
Rosewood Country Inn, *Adrian*
The Shack Country Inn, *White Cloud*
Stuart Avenue Inn, *Kalamazoo*
Victorian Villa, *Union City*

Heartland

Briaroaks Inn
Adrian

The construction of this handsome Cape Cod home began in the early 1940s, but the advent of World War II brought work to a halt. It was finally completed after the War and admired for years by local residents, including Connie and Dallas Marvin who grew up in Adrian. Located on a small hill up from the highway and encircled with trees, the home is quiet and peaceful, yet just a few minutes from the center of town. When Connie and Dallas purchased it and opened for bed-and-breakfast lodging in 1987, Connie fulfilled a longtime dream.

"I've wanted to run a B & B for years," she explained. "And I love every minute of it!"

Connie is the decorator in the family. To complement the traditional lines of the home, she selected Queen Anne cherry furnishings, wing chairs, and soft colors of rose, cream, and blue. It is a sophisticated look that blends the best of elegance and comfort.

Sparkling brass sconces light the way to the four guest rooms. Two are conveniently located on the first floor. The Country Room has a row of wooden pegs from which hang all manner of country and Amish memorabilia: hats, baskets, a lantern, handmade brooms and grapevine wreaths. In the adjacent Rose Room, guests will find a lace half-canopy over a white iron and brass bed. The second-floor Cherrywood Room has a spacious private foyer with built-in closets and drawers. With plenty of room to unpack and settle in, it is a perfect choice for extended stays. Down the hall is the romantic Antebellum Room furnished with lace curtains, a canopy bed, and a whirlpool bath for two. Each of the rooms has a private bath, TV, and phone jack.

The house backs up to a deep, wooded ravine through which runs Beaver Creek. In the spring the area is full of trillium and other wildflowers that guests in the Antebellum and Rose Rooms can enjoy from their private porches. Sliding doors at the end of the dining room offer a fine view of the area and open onto a deck where guests often like to eat breakfast in warm weather. Connie serves homemade muffins or coffee cake along with fresh fruit and juice.

"I want our guests to feel that they have had a good rest while they were here," said Connie. To that end, she serves breakfast at whatever time her guests request. Central air cools the home in summer, and a fireplace in the common room gives a cozy warmth in the winter.

"Our guests say they feel comfortable here," said Connie. "Many have never stayed in a B & B before, and when they leave, they're ready to try more!"

Vitals

rooms: 4 with private bath

pets: no

pets in residence: none

smoking: permitted in the sleeping rooms, not in the common areas

open season: year-round

rates: $42 through $69 double or single occupancy

rates include: breakfast

owners/innkeepers:

Connie and Dallas Marvin
2980 North Adrian Highway
Adrian, MI 49221
(517) 263-1659

Chicago Street Inn
Brooklyn

It was a chilly, crisp, autumn day when we visited Karen and Bill Kerr at their Chicago Street Inn. The Octoberfest was taking place in town, and Bill was laying a fire in the sitting room fireplace.

Brooklyn is a pretty little town tucked, as Karen says, "in the foothills of the Irish Hills." She describes it as growing and developing into a tourist center with good antique and craft shopping. And while Karen can bring you up to date on what is going on in the area now, Bill can tell you all about the history of Brooklyn. He grew up here. In fact, his family came from New York and settled in the area in the mid-1830s, right around the time the village was established.

"People came here because the land was plentiful and cheap," explained Bill. One person who liked the area well enough to put down roots was George Cook. He began building this Queen Anne house in 1886. George and his wife, Cora, lived there until the 1930s. The home exchanged hands five more times before the Kerrs bought it in 1986, and although it was most likely redecorated by every new owner, each preserved the lovely flower mural that Cora Cook painted in the entry way.

The home is apppointed now with a mix of antiques and country furnishings set against a background of marvelous original oak and cherry woodwork that liberally frames the windows and doors. The hearth around the sitting room fireplace is also cherry and decorated with ceramic tiles that the Cooks brought back from Europe.

In one of the sleeping rooms, you will find a matching three-piece cherry bedroom set, complemented by deep evergreen-colored carpet, matching green print wallpaper, and a rich green and peach comforter with matching pillows. By contrast, one of the smaller sleeping rooms is bright with white eyelet bedding. Still another has a marble corner sink and fine walnut furnishings. Central air-conditioning was added for extra comfort. While it all sounds elegant, and indeed, it is, Karen emphasizes that their bed-and-breakfast inn is casual and that guests are encouraged to relax and make themselves feel at home.

The Kerrs got the idea to open a bed-and-breakfast home after they stayed at the Winchester Inn in Allegan. "It made sense to me," said Karen. "We wanted a large home. Now we can have it. And by opening it as a B & B, we can share it with others."

Vitals

rooms: 4 with private bath

pets: no

pet in residence: 2 cats, not allowed in guest quarters

smoking: first floor only

open season: year-round

rates: $50 through $60 double occupancy

rates include: breakfast; rate can be lowered for guests not eating breakfast

owners/innkeepers:
Bill and Karen Kerr
219 Chicago Street
Brooklyn, MI 49230
(517) 592-3888

Clifford Lake Hotel
Stanton

On October 1, 1880, the first telegraph line was stretched from the town of Stanton to Clifford Lake six miles away. Within the next year, a post office was established and the Clifford Lake Hotel was built. A horse-drawn bus line shuttled travelers between Stanton and the hotel for fifty cents a round trip, and vacationers looked forward to riding a thirty-foot steamer that chugged around the lake.

One reporter wrote, "Clifford is becoming one of the most attractive and beautiful places of resort to be found in the state—it will eventually beat the world in progress." Life was easy and pleasures were simple.

Times changed, of course. There were two world wars, a worldwide depression, 3-D movies, and the first person in space. Through it all, the Clifford Lake Hotel endeavored to continue providing services to travelers seeking peace and quiet and good food. But it was beginning to show its age. Norm and Dyanne Eipper bought the nearly

century-old structure in 1976 and began a major renovation to turn Clifford Lake Hotel back into a comfortable lakeside inn. Their success with the project has brought vitality to the whole area, helping to keep a community and a tradition alive.

Half of the first floor of the hotel is a casual country tavern with a lot of local color. The other half is divided into several cozy dining areas that serve real good "midwestern" food. On bright Sunday mornings, diners can sit in the wide glassed-in summer porch and be treated to a bountiful country-style brunch and flooding sunshine.

The sleeping rooms upstairs are stylishly decorated with a mix of antique furniture and collectibles. They exhibit loving touches everywhere—groupings of old photos, a bowl and pitcher, and lace-trimmed pillows. Each room is named after a popular drink such as the Tequila Sunrise Room, which faces east and south and catches the morning rays. There is also a suite that sleeps four with a living room, bedroom, and full bath. Ask about the lakeside cottages that sleep from four to twelve and are available year-round by the night or for extended stays. Two have fireplaces—firewood is provided.

What would bring you to Stanton? To begin with, there is the hotel itself—a great destination point with good steaks and seafood, fresh air, and deep slumber. It is a nice place to hole up even in the dead of winter. If you feel like venturing out, you can take your pick of swimming, water-skiing, excellent fishing, an occasional pig roast, various

water sports tournaments including car races on the ice and ice golf, boating, nearby hiking, and cross-country skiing. There are three golf courses just a few minutes away and six public tennis courts at nearby Montcalm Community College. Norm and Dy also sponsor a Delta Queen Night, Summerfest, and a Fourth of July parade. If you take a drive through the rolling countryside, you will see miles and miles of the old stump fences for which Montcalm County has become so well known.

Vitals

rooms: 4 in the hotel that share 1 full bath, plus 1 suite with private bath, 4 private cottages also available

pets: no

pets in residence: none

smoking: yes

open season: year-round

rates: $45 single occupancy, $55 double occupancy in the hotel; cottages are $100 to $180 per night, $450 to $600 by the week

rates include: Continental breakfast for hotel guests

owners/innkeepers:

Dyanne and Norm Eipper
561 Clifford Lake Drive
Stanton, MI 48888   *N E of Grand Rapids*
(517) 831-5151

Hall House Bed and Breakfast
Kalamazoo

Hall House sits on a hill adjacent to Kalamazoo College, and one of the unexpected pleasures you may be treated to while staying there is the pealing of the college chapel bells. They ring out regularly in this historic neighborhood of brick streets and well-tended gardens. Henry Vander Horst designed and built Hall House as his private residence in 1923. Vander Horst was a commercial builder in the Kalamazoo area and he has left a number of fine structures, including the State Theatre, as a tribute to his skills. He spared nothing in building Hall House.

Pam and Terry O'Connor purchased the home in mid-October, 1985, and opened for bed-and-breakfast guests the following February. They have been delighted by the home's treasures, which have weathered the decades—among them, intricate moldings and a Dutch landscape on the ceiling of the library, both painted by Vander Horst when the construction business was slow.

The marble foyer with a floor of Detroit-made Pewabic tile is an example of Vander Horst's concern for quality and timeless style.

Throughout the house there is generous use of Honduras mahogany and many built-in closets and drawers . . . some with secret hiding places. An article about the Vander Horst mansion in a 1923 edition of the *Kalamazoo Gazette* (a copy is available at the inn) mentions many of the features.

Pam and Terry named the five sleeping rooms after the home's various owners and decorated each individually, in a variety of styles from contemporary to four-poster elegance. And like Vander Horst, they have paid great attention to detail.

We stayed in the O'Connor Room, originally Vander Horst's studio, which has windows facing west, south, and east. Its striking Scandinavian influence is carried out in the sleek platform bed which we found exceptionally comfortable. This room is well suited for more than two people traveling together or for those wishing to stay for several days. It is very large, with plenty of sitting room and a sofa that opens to a full-sized bed.

Down the hall is the Borgman Suite papered in a rose-colored print that sets off the well-polished brass bed. It has a private bath and an adjacent sitting room with a sofa and writing desk.

The Rutherford Room originally belonged to Vander Horst's daughter and has built-in cedar-lined closets and drawers. The O'Connors gave it a bright, informal country look, dressed it in blue and white stripes, and added a weather vane and a beautiful wooden swan. Vander Horst's own room has a queen-sized four-poster bed and a fireplace. The sleeping rooms are reached by an open stairway and a stunning landing with tall windows flanked by two of Pam's brass rubbings.

French doors off the entry lead to the dining room, where a breakfast of fresh fruit and an assortment of muffins and breads is served. The room has a graceful cove ceiling and the formality it lends was complemented during our visit by the quiet strains of classical music and a vase of calla lilies. The ballroom-sized living room has an oak floor and floor-to-ceiling windows that flood the room with morning light. Beyond it is the sun porch, furnished with white wicker.

Terry works in the international division at Upjohn and is also an auctioneer. Ask him for a demonstration! Pam says she feels like a self-appointed ambassador for Kalamazoo, and she knows firsthand the benefits of staying in bed-and-breakfast homes from her experiences in England.

Pam and Terry are proud of Kalamazoo, know the area well, and are eager to assist their guests in enjoying it. Staying at Hall House is a great way to start.

Vitals

rooms: 4 with private baths

pets: no

pets in residence: 2 parakeets in the sunroom

smoking: in the living room or sun room

open season: year-round

rates: $60 through $65 single, $65 through $70 double

rates include: breakfast

owners/innkeepers:
Pamela and Terry O'Connor
106 Thompson Street
Kalamazoo, MI 49007
(616) 343-2500

McCarthy's Bear Creek Inn
Marshall

We met Mike and Beth McCarthy several years ago when they were innkeepers at Marshall's National House Inn. They seemed well suited for the profession. Each has creative interests and artistic skills, personal warmth, and good business sense. They can talk to just about anyone about practically anything, they love Marshall, and they are adept promoters of the town's offerings. It did not surprise us to learn that they purchased their own inn in 1985 and were carrying on the tradition.

McCarthy's Bear Creek Inn is located a mile from downtown Marshall on a high, rolling, wooded parcel of land bordered by its namesake creek. The Williamsburg Cape Cod home was built in the mid-1940s by Robert Maes, a wealthy inventor of farm equipment who also fancied himself a builder of fieldstone fences. You will see his handsome stonework all about the property, connecting barns, following the hills, and bordering pastures. The fences ramble amid stately burr oaks and sugar maples, pines and spruces, and the total picture is

reminiscent of an English country estate. Mike thinks a flock of sheep grazing in the meadow would be a nice touch.

Seven sleeping rooms in the home have been decorated with a skillful mix of contemporary and antique furnishings. Some of the beautiful bedsteads are family treasures, others are reproductions that blend comfortably with wing-back chairs and watercolor paintings. The original walnut-paneled fireplace in Maes's first-floor library provides a warm, rich backdrop for a queen-sized brass bed. The Garden Room has a private entrance, and two rooms on the second floor each have a balcony from which to survey the farm. Guests staying in rooms that face Bear Creek are treated to the lulling music of water playing over smooth rocks as it makes its way through the countryside.

Last Summer, the McCarthys opened the Creek House with seven delightful sleeping rooms, including five that face Bear Creek, a sitting room, and large conference area. Located just behind the main home, the building is a former dairy barn; its stone foundation is exposed in three rooms. Among its elegant furnishings are queen-sized, four-poster beds in oak and cherry, and a log bed, all made by Michael. Each room has a set of French doors that lead to a deck or private balcony. Slate shingles used for the roof came from a supply that the McCarthys found when they moved onto the estate.

Breakfast includes a variety of breads and Michael's homemade muffins, fruits, cereals, and hard-cooked eggs. It is served in the enclosed porch, where guests can linger with a cup of coffee and yield to the pleasures of life in rural Marshall.

Vitals

rooms: 14 with private baths

pets: no

pets in residence: 1 outdoor dog

smoking: yes, except in the dining room

open season: year-round, except December 23 through 25

rates: $56 through $76 double occupancy, discounts Sunday night year-round

rates include: breakfast

owners/innkeepers:
Mike and Beth McCarthy
15230 C Drive North
Marshall, MI 49068
(616) 781-8383

The Mendon Country Inn
Mendon

The Mendon Country Inn has long been a center of activity in this tiny town and has been used for many purposes. The original structure was built in the 1840s to accommodate stagecoach travelers and later, those who passed through the area on trains. It was known as the Western Hotel. In 1873, Adams Wakeman lavishly redesigned the hotel adding eight-foot-tall windows, high ceilings, and a most graceful winding walnut staircase that will catch your attention the moment you walk in the front door.

By 1982 when Lew and Jane Kaiser bought the building, the Wakeman house had been used as a bakery, creamery, and restaurant; as a private residence; and as a place to hold community church meetings.

The Kaisers turned it back into a lodging establishment after months of extensive renovation, filling it with antiques and country furnishings.

Dick and Dolly Buerkle bought the inn in the summer of 1987. They have retained the rich country and American Indian decor that has brought the inn to the attention of national newspaper and magazine editors for the past several years. And they have added many of their own clever touches.

Each of the eleven sleeping rooms has been decorated around a theme. They vary from the cozy, informal Hired Man room to the huge first-floor Adams Wakeman room that has massive arched windows and a creekside porch. Guests will find an abundance of country memorabilia. Bright, full-sized quilts hang like giant paintings in the second

story hall, and the floors are covered with thick, richly colored rag rugs. A small, first-floor "gathering room" is filled with American Indian art.

Adjacent to the inn is a small residence that was used as the pastor's house when the inn was a church. Dick and Dolly converted it to two romantic suites that each have a queen-sized bed, full bath, fireplace, and Jacuzzi.

Dick has an extensive background in parks and recreation, and Dolly was a surgical nurse for twelve years before they became inn-keepers. Together they are developing the four-and-a-half-acre grounds of the inn into a marvelous parklike area where guests can picnic, ski, canoe, or hike in the woods and be surrounded by the area's pervasive tranquility. Bicycles and canoes are available. And the Buerkles have initiated the renaissance of the courting canoe. This custom-built version, reminiscent of those used in the late 1800s, has a special seat for the lady, who sits comfortably amid lattice and soft pillows, facing her suitor as he blithely paddles her along the river.

Breakfast is casual—usually fruit and juice, sweet things from the oven, and beverages. The large dining room can also be reserved for meetings and receptions. From the rooftop garden or the adult-sized riverside tree house, you will get a panoramic view of this beautiful countryside so peaceful and abundant in Amish and Indian tradition.

Vitals

rooms: 11 in the inn with private baths, 1 room has a sink and stool, with a shower across the hall; 2 suites with private bath and Jacuzzi.

pets: no

pets in residence: 1 dog, not allowed in sleeping quarters

smoking: in common rooms only

open season: year-round

rates: $40 through $72 double occupancy, $6 per additional person; suites $110 through $125

rates include: Continental breakfast, bicycles, and canoes from the dock

owners/innkeepers:

Dick and Dolly Buerkle
440 West Main Street
Mendon, MI 49072   S W n Battle Creek
(616) 496-8132

Mulberry House
Owosso

If you visit Mulberry House in the summer, as we did, you will be greeted by a profusion of flowers and several large gardens that dominate the grounds. They create a beautiful setting for this century-old home and provide a constant supply of cut flowers for the rooms. Jack and Carol Holmes bought Mulberry House in 1982 and worked on it for two years to produce the comfortable bed-and-breakfast you will find today. Guests have their choice of three second-floor sleeping rooms that have been furnished with casual antiques. They are papered with lovely floral prints and bear such pretty country touches as herb wreaths, potpourri hearts, and rose balls. Each has a basket of plush towels and soaps. The largest room has both a double and a single bed and is especially convenient for parents traveling with a child.

A living room on the first floor has been designed primarily for guests' use, as Jack and Carol have their own quarters. Adjacent to the living room is an elegant dining room with a plant-filled bay window and lace curtains through which streams the morning sun.

"I love to set the table with pretty dishes and fresh flowers," Carol explained. She uses crystal and china, and varies the patterns for guests staying more than one night. Breakfast includes fruit and a selection of muffins, breads, or coffee cakes, coffee, and tea.

Guests are welcome to relax on the front porch or the deck. There are many historic sites to be enjoyed in this town, and the curious Curwood Castle, built by author James Curwood, is not far. Carol can also refer you to other bed-and-breakfast homes in the area through the Bed & Breakfast in Mid-Michigan League.

Vitals

rooms: 3, 1 with private bath, 2 that share 1 bath

pets: no

pets in residence: none

smoking: in designated areas

open season: year-round

rates: $40 through $60 double occupancy

rates include: breakfast

owners/innkeepers:
Jack and Carol Holmes
1251 North Shiawassee Street
Owosso, MI 48867
(517) 723-4890

Munro House Bed and Breakfast
Jonesville

General George C. Munro built this classic Greek Revival home be-tween 1833 and 1840. Munro operated a gristmill and general store in Jonesville, but according to the county history, he was involved in extensive business both here and abroad. The home passed through Munro's family for several decades until the last of his daughters left it in 1935.

Jerry and Sandy Witt purchased the home in July, 1985, and opened it just three months later. They filled the rooms with furnishings dating from the 1800s. Most are from the Empire period, often characterized by weighty styles, claw feet, and the frequent use of rosewood, tiger and bird's-eye maple, striped satin, and featherstitching. Twelve-foot ceil-ings and interior wooden shutters add to the elegance of the first-floor living room. The five sleeping rooms are decorated individually and some of their names give a clue to the furnishings guests will find. The

Shaker Room, for example, is furnished with a reproduction Shaker trundle bed and, in the simple Shaker tradition, has pegs across one wall for hanging clothes. The ceiling in the Marshall Room is papered with a rose print that blends beautifully with pale peach carpeting and a handsome brass and bird's-eye maple bed. There are twin cannonball beds in the Stencil Room, and a huge sleigh bed in the first-floor sleeping room named for the original owner. Private sitting areas, rocking chairs, and writing desks abound. Three of the home's ten fireplaces are in sleeping rooms.

Munro's original library also has a fireplace, and a wall of built-in cupboards stocked with mugs, cups, and glasses so guests can help themselves anytime to coffee and other beverages.

Jerry and Sandy are former owners of an antique store in Saugatuck and still dabble in the business. They have done considerable work on this fine home and, with an acute respect for its history, have preserved it for decades to come. If you are looking for activities in the area, they can direct you to the Grosvenor House Museum just across the street and to a nine-hole golf course four blocks from the inn. Sandy says there are several good restaurants nearby that vary from casual to elegant to unusual. Hillsdale, with its college, is five miles away, and six

miles west on Route 12 is the tiny town of Allen with an estimated fifty antique shops.

Vitals

rooms: 5 with private baths

pets: no

pets in residence: 1 cat, seldom in guest quarters

smoking: no

open season: year-round except Christmas through New Year's

rates: $53 single, $58 double

rates include: breakfast

owners/innkeepers:
Jerry and Sandy Witt
202 Maumee Street
Jonesville, MI 49250   S w Jackson
(517) 849-9292

National House Inn
Marshall

The National House Inn opened as a stagecoach stop in 1835, two years before Michigan became a state. Like many old buildings, it has gone through several changes of use and ownership through the decades, hitting bottom as a ragged apartment house. In 1976, it was converted to a classic country inn that looks and feels as though it has been serving the needs of travelers continually, with grace and style, since before the turn of the century.

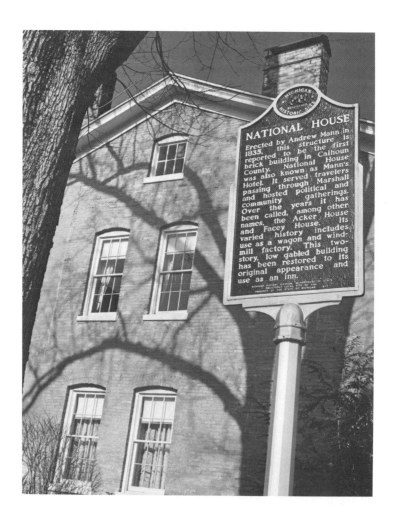

The entry room of the inn has an old plank floor and, at one end, a massive brick hearth where guests often gather. Directly above on the second floor is a large, handsome sitting room with another fireplace. There are sixteen sleeping rooms individually decorated with nineteenth-century Victorian and country-style furnishings. Some of the rooms have gleaming brass beds, while others have hand-carved wooden bedsteads with matching mirrored vanities. The linens and bedcovers are lovely and often echo the periods of decor. Three sleeping rooms occupy the main floor. All sixteen are named for Marshall's early residents, such as the elegant two-room Ketchum Suite, so named in honor of the town's founder. With the inn's choice location on the town circle, many of the rooms have a fine view of the historic Honolulu House or the Brooks Memorial Fountain. There are several common rooms on the first floor and a large country dining room where a breakfast of fruits and homemade baked goods is served. A small gift shop sells great country crafts and antique reproductions.

Innkeeper Barbara Bradley has had the pleasure of welcoming guests from all over the world and from many backgrounds. Through-

out the year she schedules special afternoon teas with guest speakers who lecture on such topics as herb use and antique linens. The inn also hosts weekend programs including candlelight tours through some of the city's most famous homes. Barbara writes a delightful newsletter that features a schedule of upcoming events at the inn, highlights of past months, and some time-tested recipes.

There is much to see and do at the National House, as well as in this historic town that once thought it would surely be chosen as Michigan's capital. Antique shops abound, and architectural history connoisseurs will find it a paradise.

Vitals

rooms: 16, each has a private bath

pets: no

pets in residence: none

smoking: yes, but discouraged in the dining room

open season: year-round except Christmas Eve and Christmas Day

rates: $55 through $89 double occupancy, $6 for third person in the same room

rates include: breakfast

innkeeper:
Barbara Bradley
102 South Parkview
Marshall, MI 49068
(616) 781-7374

The Old Lamp-Lighter's Homestay
Battle Creek

This home is quite possibly one of the purest examples of Arts and Crafts architecture you will find in the state. The style was popular for only a short time in the early part of this century and provided a sort of bridge from the elegance of turn-of-the century Victorian to the clean, practical lines of Frank Lloyd Wright's Prairie School. There are details to look for in Arts and Crafts design, and you will see them all at this lovely bed-and-breakfast home.

The building of this structure began in 1909 but it was not finished until 1914. In fact, the original builders sold the house to Seirn and Elizabeth Cole in 1913 and never had the opportunity to live there. Cole was a prominent building contractor in Battle Creek. Among his accomplishments are the Post School, the Ralston Purina building, and City Hall. He was also a charter member of the Battle Creek Chamber of Commerce and a 1933 candidate for mayor. The Coles lived in the home until 1917 when they sold it to George and Dora Rich, but several

years later when the Riches moved to California, the Coles bought it back.

By the time Roberta Stewart saw the home in 1986, it was overgrown with evergreens and so dark inside that she asked to come back and see it on a bright, sunny day. To her surprise, the sunlight revealed elaborate Gothic stenciling throughout the foyer, a hand-painted mural on all four walls of the dining room, and two pairs of stained-glass French doors that repeat the theme of the mural. And that was just the start.

The brick exterior is trimmed with copper porch roofs and gutters, cut limestone, and stucco and timber gables that exemplify a Tudor influence. Inside you will find Gothic-style arched doors and ample use of rich, quarter-sawn oak and Honduras mahogany. Roberta added oriental rugs and Dutch lace curtains to match the elegance of the home's built-in features such as leaded windows and signed Steuben light fixtures. The large living room and cozy library both have a fireplace.

There are four bedrooms on the second floor including a small one that adjoins the W. K. Kellogg Room. The latter is a perfect setup for families traveling with children or for two couples. Three bedrooms on the third floor are more casually furnished. The large Sands McCamly

Room, also called the family room, sleeps six people comfortably and has an area with a table and chairs so children can spread out games and toys and play without disturbing others. All the sleeping rooms have ceiling fans and cable TV. Some are air-conditioned.

Guests are served a full breakfast together at a great round table in the muraled dining room. There's always a hot entrée as well as choices of dry cereal, juice and fruit, muffins, and a whole drawer full of teas. We had a baked pancake on one occasion and rich, walnut-and-cream-cheese-stuffed French toast on another. Both were excellent.

There is a lot to see and do in Battle Creek, and Roberta or her sister-in-law Evelyn can point you in the right direction. Ask about the special golf and cross-country skiing packages that are available to you as her guest. And consider the Old Lamp-Lighter's if you are in Battle Creek on business. Roberta will adjust the breakfast hour so you can make your earliest appointments.

Vitals

rooms: 7, most with private baths

pets: no

pets in residence: 1 dog

smoking: outside only

open season: year-round

rates: $45 through $60 double occupancy, family room is $75

rates include: full breakfast

owner/innkeeper:
> Roberta Stewart
> 276 Capital Avenue N.E.
> Battle Creek, MI 49017
> (616) 963-2603

River Haven
White Pigeon

Jim and Blanche Pressler live in a lovely brick ranch-style home on a bank above the St. Joseph River. Situated just a few miles north of the Michigan-Indiana state line, their home is surrounded by lush orderly farms and is close to Amish communities, flea markets, and the renowned Shipshewana auctions. They call it River Haven.

In keeping with the flavor of the area, this bed and breakfast home is filled with country furnishings, crafts, and family memorabilia. The beds in each of the three guest rooms are covered with custom Amish-made quilts and pillows in traditional patterns. Our room was decorated in blues and accented by a quilt that was pieced in shades of an early morning summer sky. Some of the rugs and furnishings have been made by the Presslers' Amish friends and may be purchased or custom ordered. Jim urged us to try out a pair of Amish-made rocking chairs that were new since our first visit. They were fashioned of slats and

branches, with the branches used like bentwood, and were remarkably comfortable.

Jim, it seems, can do anything well, but his skills are most immediately obvious in the large gardens all around the home. He grows a variety of flowers, fruits, and vegetables in the rich river valley soil, and his love for the river is apparent. Sometimes he and Blanche get up very early in the morning and sit on their back porch just to listen to the rest of the world waking up. "We come out here and listen to the fish flopping and the birds starting to sing and the rooster crowing on the other bank," Jim explained. "The river is full of life at that time."

Blanche is an accomplished cook and baker. Her delicious rolls and breads are offered to River Haven guests in the morning when they

gather around the big dining room table to enjoy a hearty breakfast. Blanche also provides lots of little "extras" such as the lemonade and cookies we received on arrival.

River Haven is a warm, relaxed, quietly Christian home. The Presslers are kind, gentle people with a gift for easy conversation and a genuine ability to make their guests feel welcome.

Vitals

rooms: 3 sleeping rooms, 1 with a private bath, 2 share a full bath and a half

pets: no

pets in residence: none

smoking: not in the house, but guests are welcome to join Jim outside

open season: year-round

rates: $35 single, $45 double, $10 each additional person

rates include: full breakfast

owners/innkeepers:
Blanche and Jim Pressler
9222 St. Joe River Road
White Pigeon, MI 49099
(616) 483-9104

Rosewood Country Inn
Adrian

You will find the Rosewood Country Inn at the end of a long driveway that meanders through old stands of pine and hardwoods. The original portion of the structure was built during the late 1800s, and at the turn of the century it was part of a 160-acre working farm with a thriving dairy business. In 1950, Dr. Howard Heffron purchased the farm and remodeled the home, adding three wings and supplying the Williamsburg influence that is still evident today. He was also responsible for extensive plantings, including many fruit trees, that give the grounds a parklike quality. Innkeepers Pat and Don Rose took us for a walk around the estate and pointed out some of the unusual trees, such as the sweet gum, that Heffron cultivated.

The Roses bought this marvelous country home, with ten acres, in April, 1985, and opened for bed-and-breakfast guests the following September. They used colonial-style furnishings, including wing-back chairs and braided rugs on hardwood floors, to play up the traditional

lines of the home. There are touches of country-folk decor but always used sparingly to enhance the clean, uncluttered look. The sleeping rooms are large and bright, furnished with antiques and decorated with a predominance of blues and white. The total effect is simple country elegance. We had not seen it so well done before and were quite taken with it.

A Continental breakfast of muffins or rolls, fruits and juice, and specialty coffees is served during the week at the guests' convenience to accommodate those who have to make early-morning meetings or business appointments. On the weekends, breakfast is set up in the dining room, just off the expansive living room.

Pat and Don both attended nearby Adrian College. Don is an elementary school principal and Pat is a former teacher. They are a delightful couple and, along with their children, Julie and Brian, spread much warmth throughout this inn.

Vitals

rooms: 4, 2 with private baths

pets: no

pets in residence: none

smoking: yes, except in sleeping rooms

open season: year-round

rates: $38 through $48 double occupancy

rates include: Continental breakfast

owners/innkeepers:
> Don and Pat Rose
> 3325 South Adrian Highway (M-52)
> Adrian, MI 49221
> (517)263-5085

The Shack Country Inn
White Cloud

Janette and Marv Deur were both born and raised within ten miles of the Shack and bought it in 1976. The name of this inn is misleading. It is actually a very large and well-built log lodge constructed in 1945 from trees that grew in a stand seven miles east of the property. It sits on 75 acres of meadow and woods and overlooks 120-acre Robinson Lake. This is the second log structure to occupy the land. The first was built in the early 1900s but it burned down in 1942. It was called the Shack, and the name has stuck. The present lodge was constructed by a furniture dealer from Grand Rapids who, apparently not wanting this log structure to suffer the same fate as the first, added built-in fire hoses and a water-pumping system.

The lodge has a huge first-floor living room with groupings of comfortable couches and chairs, a built-in TV, a pool table, and a fireplace. A bow window spans one end of the room, affording a great view of the lake. Paintings and prints, antiques, oil lamps, collections of

dishes and knickknacks are found throughout the lodge—many against the backdrop of smooth lacquered logs that lend a warm, homey feeling. And always there is the unmistakably delicious scent of wood mingling with whatever good things Janette is baking.

At this writing the Shack has six good-sized sleeping rooms with private baths. The Deurs are planning to expand in 1989 and add another twenty rooms plus a dining area that will seat one hundred, and a meeting room in the basement. Guests will continue to be treated to a big, country breakfast with eggs, bacon or sausage, toast, cereal, juice and coffee. The menu varies for guests staying more than one night and will often include pancakes or French toast with maple syrup from the Deurs' own sugar bush. Ice cream is served for an evening snack!

There is a sandy beach just in front of the lodge, and Marv says the fishing in Robinson Lake is above average. Anglers routinely pull in large- and small-mouth bass, pike, bluegill, and perch. Many are also successful at spear fishing. Guests have the use of a fishing boat, canoe, and paddleboats at no extra charge. Lodge guests are often members of a wedding party or those gathering for family or class reunions. "This is a good place for quiet adult relaxation," Marv explained.

There is plenty of room to picnic and play games on the lawn.

Within easy driving distance are two golf courses. If you plan a spring visit, you may want to time your stay to coincide with the tapping of the maple trees. Janette and Marv, with the help of their children, produce about seventy gallons of syrup during a good season, and you will be welcome to help carry the sap buckets. It is an exhilarating springtime tradition and a lot of fun.

Vitals

rooms: 6, 3 have private baths with showers, 3 have private lavatories with a stool and sink and 1 shared shower (20 with private baths due to open in 1989)

pets: no

pets in residence: none

smoking: yes; nonsmoking areas and nonsmoking rooms are available

open season: year-round

rates: $30 single, $40 and $45 for a couple in 1 bed, $42 for a couple in 2 beds, $7.50 per additional person in same room

rates include: breakfast and evening ice cream

owners/innkeepers:

Marv and Janette Deur
2263 West 14th Street
White Cloud, MI 49349
(616) 924-6683   *NW Grand Rapids*

Stuart Avenue Inn
Kalamazoo

There was a lot of money in Kalamazoo at the turn of the century, and the city has several blocks of mansions in various states of repair to prove it. One of the area's first wealthy residents was U.S. Senator Charles Stuart, who built an Italianate villa on the outskirts of the business district in 1854. Few others moved in around him because only the wealthiest could afford a private horse and buggy to ride to work in town each day. In the 1880s, the horse-drawn trolleys were put on the streets making the exclusive neighborhood more accessible. By the 1890s, the Stuart neighborhood was filled with magnificent architecture representing several periods.

One of the homes was a large Queen Anne residence on Stuart Avenue built by Frank Cowgill in 1889. It was described in a history of Kalamazoo as having achieved a timeless serenity.

Young James Balch came to the progressive river town of Kalama-

zoo to attend Kalamazoo College. He married, became a successful businessman, and eventually served three terms as mayor of Kalamazoo during World War I. Balch and his wife, Mabel, bought the Queen Anne home from Frank Cowgill's widow and lived there for half a century.

By the time Bill and Andrea (Andy) Casteel bought the home in July, 1983, it had been divided into apartments. They spent a lot of time "undoing" and then began restoring the building with the kind of determined spirit that is spreading through the historic neighborhood. They opened their doors as a bed-and-breakfast home three months later.

There are six sleeping rooms available to guests. All are beautifully decorated and furnished in the style of the late 1800s with bold, Victorian reproduction wallpaper and fine antiques. Most of the bedsteads are handsome reproductions in queen size. Two of the rooms have fireplaces and one also has a small kitchen and private entrance. Each room has a private bath, cable TV, and a telephone.

The Eastlake sitting room on the second floor is open to all guests. It is a wonderful place to sit and read or gather with others to share a

bottle of wine before dinner. Croissants and sweet cakes are served for breakfast in the main-floor dining room—one of the cheeriest we have seen. The morning light streams in through ten windows. Stroll around the grounds of the home and you will see some of the work that Andy and Bill put into re-creating a turn-of-the-century look outside. You will also find their traditional rose garden in bloom throughout the summer.

Bill retired from Kalamazoo's Upjohn Company and is a partner in the West Hills Athletic Club. If you are up early enough, you may be able to join him for a run around the Stuart neighborhood. He and Andy are both delightful company.

We recommend Stuart Avenue especially to business travelers and to those for whom bed-and-breakfast lodging is a new experience. If you are planning an extended stay in the Kalamazoo area, ask about the other historic homes that Bill and Andy have renovated in the neighborhood including the Bartlett-Upjohn House just a few doors away. They are available for single-night or short-term rental and offer surroundings similar to the inn.

Vitals

rooms: 6, all with private baths; Melinda's Room also has a small kitchen and a separate entrance

pets: no

pets in residence: 1 dog, not allowed in sleeping rooms

smoking: not permitted in the house

open season: year-round

rates: $45 through $55 for a single, double occupancy is $5 additional, weekly rates available

rates include: breakfast

owners/innkeepers:
  Bill and Andrea Casteel
  405 Stuart Avenue
  Kalamazoo, MI 49007
  (616) 342-0230

Victorian Villa
Union City

The Victorian Villa is as much a living lesson in Victorian history and culture as it is a romantic bed-and-breakfast inn. This magnificent structure was commissioned to be built in 1872 by Dr. William P. Hurd and completed four years later at a cost of twelve thousand dollars. Craftsmen who erected the ornate home worked for as little as eight cents a day.

Dr. Hurd had come to Union City from Genesee County, New York, several years earlier to join his brothers in a medical practice. He also became founder and chairman of the National Bank of Union City. But

in 1881, after living in his Victorian mansion for only five years, Dr. Hurd died of a kidney ailment. Caroline Hobard Hurd, whom the doctor had wed in 1842, continued to live in the home until her death in 1910. In 1950, the mansion was converted to apartments.

Ron Gibson first discovered the villa in the early 1970s, but he had to wait for seven years—persistent, eager, and full of grand plans—until the owner would sell it. His first task, assisted by his wife, Sue, was to undo several decades of "modernization." You will find the home now, like a tiny museum, filled with the lace and finery, crystal, oil paintings, parlor plants, printed wallpaper, and furniture that exemplify various periods of the Victorian era. Everywhere you look you will see

the quality of workmanship that was built into the remarkable home more than one hundred years ago.

The eight bedchambers are each distinctively decorated in a popular style of the 1800s and named for the periods they represent. They begin with 1840s Empire and continue with Rococo, Renaissance, Eastlake, and Edwardian. The second-floor Victorian Country Suite has a viewing balcony overlooking the estate gardens. On the third floor are two Victorian Tower suites that share an adjoining parlor.

Although there are antique shops and great pastoral scenes within an easy drive of Victorian Villa, we classify this jewel as a destination inn—a place were you can go to imbibe the gentle side of life. Ron has observed, "People often come here to get away from everything else. They come to celebrate special occasions. For some it's a time just to get reacquainted, a time to fall in love again."

Accommodations at Victorian Villa include an afternoon beverage that varies depending on the season, and an extended Continental breakfast. At a guest's request, Ron can make arrangements for champagne or wine, hors d'oeuvres, and flowers. Ask about the sumptuous twelve-item Victorian tea that will be served by reservation in the afternoon or early evening. It has a varying menu that includes madeleines, Battenburg cakes, crumpets, and scones with jams made from the fruits in the Victorian-styled gardens that surround the inn. Special old-fashioned Victorian weekends are planned throughout the year. Victorian Christmas weekends held from Thanksgiving through New Year's will give you the opportunity to partake in the roast goose and plum pudding, magic shows, caroling, and wassail of a nineteenth century holiday. New to the repertoire are Sherlock Holmes Mystery weekends and Summer Daze weekends, complete with candlelight croquet and ice-cream churning.

Vitals

rooms: 8 sleeping rooms, 6 have private baths, 2 share 1 bath

pets: no

pets in residence: none

smoking: not permitted inside

open season: year-round

rates: $55 through $70 single, $60 through $75 double occupancy

rates include: breakfast and afternoon beverage

owners/innkeepers:

Ron and Sue Gibson
601 North Broadway
Union City, MI 49094   S ∩ marshall
(517) 741-7383

Metro

The Botsford Inn, *Farmington Hills*
Boulevard Inn, *Tecumseh*
Country Heritage Bed and Breakfast, *Romeo*
Country Inn of Grand Blanc, *Grand Blanc*
Governor's Inn, *Lexington*
The Homestead, *Saline*
Mayflower Hotel, *Plymouth*
Montague Inn, *Saginaw*
Murphy Inn, *St. Clair*
Oakbrook Inn, *Davison*
Raymond House Inn, *Port Sanilac*
Vickie Van's Bed and Breakfast, *Lexington*
The Victorian Inn, *Port Huron*
Wood's Inn, *Ann Arbor*

The Botsford Inn
Farmington Hills

"This was Henry Ford's own furniture," John Anhut said as we stood in an alcove of the living room at the Botsford Inn. He ran his hand gently over the back of a tall rocker and across the polished surface of a round wooden table. John's reverence for Ford is obvious. And after thirty-eight years as owner and keeper of the inn that for a time belonged to the benevolent millionaire, he still seems awed by it all.

There are different versions of what led to Henry Ford's purchasing the inn. The most frequently told is that he was courting his wife-to-be, Clara, the first time he saw it. Out of that nostalgia, Ford bought the inn and restored it.

That was in the early 1920s and the building and business were already eighty years old. The original structure had been built by Orrin Weston in 1836 to be a private home. Five years later, Stephen Jennings

THE BOTSFORD INN

This historic inn, the oldest in Michigan still providing food and lodging, was built as a home in 1836 by Orrin Weston. In 1841 it was converted into a tavern by Stephen Jennings. Known as the Sixteen Mile House, it was the stagecoach stop here in Clarenceville on the Grand River plank road, which followed an Indian trail that went on to Lake Michigan. Milton C. Botsford in 1860 acquired the inn. It became a popular meeting place for drovers, farmers, and travelers to and from Detroit. Henry Ford, who had first seen the inn while courting his future wife, Clara, in a horse and buggy, purchased the inn from the Botsfords in 1924 and restored it. The Fords operated it until 1951.

bought it and turned it into a general store and very popular tavern called the 16 Mile House. Located on what was then the Grand River Trail, it served as a convenient stop along the Lansing-Detroit stage-coach route.

In 1860, it was sold again, this time to Milton Botsford who gave the inn his name. The Botsfords held frequent dances in the ballroom and, on one fortuitous evening, young Henry Ford and Clara Bryant attended. Ford bought the inn in 1924 and started pouring money into it . . . hundreds of thousands of dollars over a period of just a few years. He also moved it back from the main road about three hundred feet and put new footings under it.

John Anhut purchased the inn from Ford's estate in 1951. Since that

time, three additions have been built that are so skillfully designed and furnished it is difficult to tell where the old stops and the new begins.

The theme is Early American from the wooden bedsteads and wing-back chairs in the sleeping rooms to the turkey and dressing and chicken potpies on the dinner menu. The heavy, supporting ceiling beams and smooth, old wooden floors in the original section will take you back to the time when Detroit was a full day's carriage ride from the inn. You will see fine furnishings that were collected from around the world and placed in the Botsford by Henry and Clara years ago. Yet, in a striking blend of the old and the new, you will also find such modern amenities as tennis courts, in-room coffee, TVs, hair driers, and an automatic wake-up service. The feeling here is warm and inviting, and the sense of tradition is strong.

Vitals

rooms: 68 rooms, all with private baths

pets: no

pets in residence: none

smoking: yes

open season: year-round

rates: $45 and $55 single, $62 and 70 double, $85 through $110 suites

rates include: full, prepared-to-order breakfast

owner/innkeeper:
    John Anhut
    28000 Grand River
    Farmington Hills, MI 48024
    (313) 474-4800

Boulevard Inn
Tecumseh

The original section of this sturdy old home was a simple Greek Revival structure built in 1852 for Henry and Elizabeth Bacon who farmed the contiguous eighty acres. Twenty-five years later, owner Robert Cairns commissioned builder Salmon Crane to put a sizable Italianate addition onto the front of the house, which accounts for the beautiful edifice you see now as you pass on West Chicago Boulevard.

In 1985, Gary and Judy Hicks bought the aging structure and then hit on the idea of turning it into a bed-and-breakfast inn. Although it was in great need of repair and rebuilding, the project caught the interest of members of the Tecumseh Area Historical Society who selected the Boulevard Inn to be their 1986 Designer House. It was one of the last salvageable homes in the area, the others having yielded to commercial development.

"Nearly everybody in town knew about the house and many were willing to help," added Judy. "We started by stripping the walls to the

studs. Then we worked with the carpenters to put the new walls in the right places."

Later, when the decorating began, the designers used colors, fabrics, and wall coverings to interpret Judy's descriptions of how she wanted the rooms to feel. While the bulk of the restoration fell to Judy and Gary, 120 volunteers lent their time and skills to help sand, scrape, clean, paper, and paint. Merchants and business people contributed some of the materials at a discount. Friends brought food for the workers. Fifteen-hour workdays were not uncommon. The resulting look was elegant, uncluttered Victorian with lots of details to catch and delight the eye. And it was all completed with hours to spare for the historical society's celebration "Promenade the Past" on May 16, 1986.

There are eight sleeping rooms from which guests may choose. The Robert Cairns Room and Beland Room on the first floor exemplify the formal Victorian style with high bedsteads, and marble-topped dressers and tables. Both have a private bath. The three second-floor rooms toward the back of the house are carpeted and have pretty printed papers on the walls and dormer ceilings. The three front rooms are more spacious, including the Master Suite with its two-person Jacuzzi, private sitting room, and "Twin-hearts" iron and brass bed.

We were entranced with the marvelous deep wine color Judy selected for the parlor walls and the early nineteenth-century technique called scumbling that was used to make them look like leather. They are bordered with a beautiful Lincrusta Walton frieze, a type of heavy, embossed wallpaper that replicates those produced around the turn of the century. Another pattern is used as a wainscotting with forest green in the adjacent dining room. Quite spectacular.

After breakfast—ours was delicious and ample—a stroll outside along a brick garden path will take you to a gazebo and give you a view of the lovely grounds that have been developed in the past two years. Tucked back from the busy road, this house is a tiny Victorian oasis where you can slow the pace for awhile, yet be close to stores, restaurants, and all the conveniences of the twentieth century.

In addition to innkeeping, Judy conducts communication seminars that are offered to businesses and individuals. You can ask her for more information about training seminars and retreats that are scheduled at the inn.

Vitals

rooms: 8, 6 with private bath, 2 share 1 bath

pets: no

pets in residence: 2 cats

smoking: no

open season: year-round

rates: $60 through $110 double occupancy

rates include: full breakfast

owners/innkeepers:

　　Judy and Gary Hicks
　　904 West Chicago Boulevard
　　Tecumseh, MI 49286
　　(517) 423-5169

Country Heritage Bed and Breakfast
Romeo

When we visited Country Heritage one August afternoon, we were greeted by innkeeper Jo Ann Celani, a peacock named Arthur, and the aroma of freshly baked peach cobbler. The Romeo area is noted for its peaches, Jo Ann explained, and she was making dessert for guests to enjoy later that evening. She usually takes it to their rooms before bedtime.

Jo Ann and her husband, George, bought this historic 1840s Greek Revival home in 1978. They have filled it with a wonderful collection of heirlooms and country memorabilia. "I've always loved the old and the antique," Jo Ann remembers. "I was born in an old farmhouse in Ohio and even as a young girl I was always bringing home crocks and treasured finds."

In 1986, they opened for bed and breakfast lodging because, Jo Ann wrote us, " . . . this is a very charming farm and too lovely not to share."

Guest accommodations include three antique-furnished second-floor guest rooms, and a romantic suite on the first floor that has a fireplace in the sitting room and bedroom and a footed tub in the private bath. It is the favorite of honeymooners who often return to celebrate their anniversaries. You will find hand-crocheted lace on many of the linens and quilts on all the beds. The beautiful five-plait braided rugs were made by Jo Ann's uncle. In the evening and on gloomy days, electric candles light each window of the home. The ambience is warm, peaceful, and cheerful.

Breakfast includes fresh fruit and juice, beverages, and "something from the oven," such as blueberry, bran, or peach muffins baked by the Celanis' daughter, Jill. She is also an accomplished craftswoman and

interior designer, with a successful needlework shop in town called "Home Stitch Home."

In this tranquil setting, the Celanis have hosted executives from Japan, Mexico, England, and Canada who enjoy an escape from the noise and fast pace of the city. There are six acres to wander and a swimming pool for hot summer days. In addition to the fireplaces in the suite, there are two in the common rooms and George keeps them stoked when the temperature drops. Jo Ann says the home is especially nice at Christmas with the fires ablaze and the rooms dressed up with the look of an old-fashioned holiday.

Vitals

rooms: 4, 2 have private baths, 2 share 1 full bath

pets: no

pets in residence: 1 peacock and 1 hen who will not come inside

smoking: no

open season: year-round

rates: $50 through $70 double occupancy

rates include: breakfast

owners/innkeepers:

Jo Ann and George Celani
64707 Mound Road
Romeo, MI 48065
(313) 752-2879

Country Inn of Grand Blanc
Grand Blanc

Neva and Earl Pigeon had the good fortune to live in Spain for four years through Earl's work with General Motors. On weekends, they traveled extensively throughout the European countryside staying in bed-and-breakfast homes. They so enjoyed the bed-and-breakfast experiences that they decided to open their own home when they returned to the States.

In 1985, they purchased a stately brick Victorian residence built at the turn of the century by a prominent Grand Blanc judge. It is reached by a long, tree-lined drive, and encircled by flowers and neatly pruned hedges. A few well-kept barns and outbuildings remain from the days when this estate was a working farm.

The main entrance to the home takes you into the warming room where a corner fireplace burns cozily on frosty days. The common areas and three second-floor sleeping rooms contain an attractive mix of antique and contemporary furnishings. For special occasions, Neva says most guests choose the Suite with its lace-covered king-sized bed and

pretty peaches-and-cream decor. It has a small sitting room with a romantic ruffle and pillow-covered daybed, a TV and VCR, and a skirted table for two. If guests prefer breakfast in their room, Neva delivers it in one of her hand-painted picnic baskets.

The Rose Room has a queen-sized bed and is papered with a whimsical flower print on a black background. It shares a bath with a snug, third-floor room called the Loft—the quietest spot in the house and a treasured getaway, according to Neva. Its guests have the use of a large second-floor sitting room that families or couples traveling together can share when they rent both the Loft and the Rose Room. Guests will find a complimentary bottle of champagne in their room on arrival—the same brand that Earl and Neva enjoyed in Spain.

Breakfast here includes croissants with homemade jams, juice, fresh fruit in season, and blended coffee. We sampled the fragrant chocolate-raspberry coffee that Neva serves with a sweetened, whipped topping and it was marvelous.

If you are interested in a hot-air balloon ride, ask Earl and Neva about the package they offer in conjunction with the nearby Balloon Corporation of American. "We get a lot of guests here who are having their first balloon ride *and* their first experience staying in a bed-and-breakfast home," Neva told us.

Business travelers should note that General Motors is just fifteen minutes away. There is a vineyard in nearby Holly, good golfing at the Grand Blanc Country Club, and excellent cross-country skiing through-out the area, including the ten-acre grounds of the inn.

Vitals

rooms: 3, 1 with a private bath, 2 that share 1 bath

pets: no

pets in residence: none

smoking: designated areas, discouraged in sleeping rooms

rates: $45 through $65 double occupancy

rates include: Continental breakfast, complimentary champagne

open season: year-round

owners/innkeepers:

    Earl and Neva Pigeon
    6136 South Belsay Road
    Grand Blanc, MI 48439
    (313) 694-6749

Governor's Inn
Lexington

This handsome residence was built as a private home in 1859 by Charles Moore. At that time, Lexington was a major Great Lakes port. The trains carrying Michigan lumber bound for shipping ended at Lexington's docks, so pine was readily available and used extensively for the home's construction. The builder added a touch of elegance in the carved stairway and oak carpenter's lace, but otherwise the interior would have been considered quite simple in its day. The exterior is a different story, however, demonstrating several architectural styles including Italianate, Greek Revival, and Carpenter's Gothic.

On July 30, 1901, Charles Moore's youngest daughter, Mary, was married at the home to aspiring politician Albert (Bert) E. Sleeper, who became Michigan's governor in 1917. The Sleepers spent several summers there, where porch sitting and the simple life of a small town provided a retreat from the political spotlight.

Many decades later, the residence—now a bed-and-breakfast home—is still very much a "summer place." Jane and Bob MacDonald have furnished the inn and its three sleeping rooms with cotton rugs and Haywood-Wakefield wicker, iron beds, and light colored linens. Lace and eyelet curtains span many of the nearly floor-to-ceiling windows, yielding gracefully to the breezes off Lake Huron. The lines are clean, fresh, and uncluttered.

Continental breakfast is served in the first floor dining room at a great old table large enough to seat all the guests. But for those who wish, the fresh fruit and sweet cakes may also be eaten outside on the wraparound porch.

Lexington seems yet undiscovered by summer travelers. And that is only one of the reasons to come visit this quiet harbor town. Boaters

and anglers will find clean waters, great fishing, and a state-maintained marina. Lake Huron sailing is superb.

Jane and Bob know that many of their guests come to Lexington to get away from everything else. They have private living quarters in the inn and have developed a sixth sense for knowing when visitors want to chat and when they want to be alone. You will find them to be gracious hosts.

Vitals

rooms: 3 sleeping rooms, each with private bath

pets: no

pets in residence: none

smoking: first floor only

open season: Memorial Day through September

rates: $40 for 2 persons, room air conditioner available for $15

rates include: Continental breakfast

owners/innkeepers:

Jane and Bob MacDonald
P.O. Box 471
Lexington, MI 48450
(313) 359-5770

The Homestead
Saline

If you remember the spring of 1986, you may remember the end of May, when it rained for seven days straight. We arrived at the Homestead on the eighth day under clear skies and found the season in full bloom. Cedar waxwings, barn swallows, and eastern orioles were in abundance. Trumpet vine and peony bushes were going through their decades-old ritual of sprouting fat buds. Trilliums and other wildflowers planted by Shirley Grossman, owner and innkeeper of the Homestead, were already bending under the weight of their blooms.

Shirley has occupied this farm estate since 1963, and although the home was built in 1851, her family was only the third to own it. They purchased it, furnished, from the Smith family, and among the treasures they received was a steamer chest full of arrowheads picked up in the surrounding fields by the elder Mr. Smith. This valley is rich in Indian history. The Saline River flows through the back of Shirley's property; it

was on its banks that the Indians used to set up camp to salt and preserve their fish, making use of the natural salt wells found throughout the area. It is from the wells that the river and city take their name. Michigan Avenue, just a mile north, was the east-west trail running between Detroit and Chicago.

Shirley raised five children in this home, and in 1984 she opened for bed-and-breakfast guests. Her six sleeping rooms are furnished with antiques and family heirlooms, including canopy and walnut bedsteads. Many of the furnishings belonged to the original owners. There is a comfortable mix here of turn-of-the-century elegance and the relaxed informality of a home that has been lived in and enjoyed for many decades and by many generations.

Shirley brings out crackers and cheese for guests in the early eve-

ning, which gives everyone a good opportunity to meet and mingle in the living room and parlor. She also keeps a steady supply of books, magazines, and daily newspapers on hand for her guests. Those who can play a tune are welcome to try their hand at the upright piano. The home has central heat, but wood-burning stoves in the parlor and dining room add to the coziness on cold days.

A full breakfast is served, with the offerings varying each day. We enjoyed dilled eggs and hot popovers with a selection of jellies and jams. The table was dressed with a soft pink lace cloth, fresh flowers, and candles. And each place was set with individual salt and pepper cellars. It was delightful.

If you are looking for shopping, music, theater, and dining, you can be in Ann Arbor or Ypsilanti in about fifteen minutes, and the town of Saline is just a half mile north.

Vitals

rooms: 6, 5 that share that share 2 full baths, 1 with a private bath
pets: no
pets in residence: outdoor cats
smoking: yes
open season: year-round
rates: $26 through $60
rates include: breakfast
owner/innkeeper:
    Shirley Grossman
    9279 Macon Road
    Saline, MI 48176
    (313) 429-9625

Mayflower Hotel
Plymouth

Ralph Lorenz began working at the Mayflower Hotel in 1939, and that is where you will still find him today. The hotel was built in 1927 as the joint venture of Plymouth's Rotary and Kiwanis clubs and the Chamber of Commerce. It was their hope that the Mayflower would serve as a focal point for town activities, and with Ralph's guidance for more than forty-five years, it has. In 1964, he and his wife, Mabel, seized an opportunity to purchase the hotel. In 1981, Ralph received the Small Business Association's National Senior Advocate of the Year Award for his leadership and contributions in the city of Plymouth. It was bestowed by then Vice-President George Bush in the Rose Garden of the White House.

Located in the heart of this progressive community, the Mayflower has for decades been a source of innovative ideas. Years ago, it led the way in hospitality trends such as in-room air-conditioning and TVs. In the early 1970s, Ralph was inspired by a trip overseas to institute a bed-and-breakfast plan, and his tongue-in-cheek reason still makes guests

chuckle . . . "More people eat than swim, so we included breakfast with the room instead of putting in a pool."

The hotel is flavored Early American and Colonial, with a nautical motif carried through in the pub and dining rooms. There is a feeling of warm elegance throughout the hotel along with an unprecedented friendliness offered by the employees, many of whom have worked at the hotel for several years, and by family members who have been raised in the business.

Guest accommodations are located in both the original hotel and in a thirty-nine-room motor-hotel-style addition called the Mayflower II. The rooms are large and all one hundred received a facelift this past winter. Those in the hotel have been redecorated with four-poster beds and antique reproductions to give the flavor of a country inn. Several were outfitted with two-person Jacuzzis. All rooms have direct-dial phones, color TV, and private bathrooms. Guests staying in the May-flower II also have refrigerators.

The food is as good as the hotel boasts. Among their innovative offerings are fine vintage European and American wines that can be served by the glass, thanks to the steward's use of Michigan's first nitro-gen wine preservation system, called a Cruvinet. The complimentary

breakfast is a full meal—guests have their choice of eggs, pancakes, bacon or sausages, cereals, and beverages.

In 1983, son Scott, who is now the hotel's general manager, implemented the brilliant idea of a par value program in the hotel, giving visiting Canadians face value for their Canadian dollars. The hotel is ideally suited to tour groups and the staff makes them feel welcome immediately on arrival by rolling out an actual red carpet.

Across from the hotel is the town square, site of dances, art fairs, band concerts, and the nationally known ice sculpture spectacular. If you want to plan your visit to coincide with a truly breath-taking event, ask about the Mayflower's annual hot-air balloon festival held each July. Within minutes of the hotel, you can watch the horses race at Northville Downs and select from seven golf courses. Less than half an hour away are Ann Arbor, Metro Airport, Greenfield Village, Tiger Stadium, and the Renaissance Center.

Vitals

rooms: 100 with private baths; some also have a private whirlpool

pets: no

pets in residence: none

smoking: yes

open season: year-round

rates: $59 through $85 single, $62.50 through $125 double, children under 10 free if in same room with adults

rates include: full breakfast

owners/innkeepers:
Scott Lorenz
Randy Lorenz
Creon Smith
827 West Ann Arbor Trail
Plymouth, MI 48170
(313) 453-1620

Montague Inn
Saginaw

This magnificent Georgian-style mansion was built for the Montague family in 1929. Among its numerous outstanding original features are half-a-dozen Art Deco tiled baths, built-in library bookshelves with secret passages, pegged oak floors, and deep bay windows. But perhaps the most incredible aspect of this home is that it was built for a family of four. Its full size is not apparent from the street because a long wing that extends from the back of the home is not visible from the front. That was a trend in design during the Depression, presumably because the owners did not wish to flaunt their wealth. If you step out to the back gardens, take a brief stroll toward Lake Linton, and turn to face the home again, you will be better able to appreciate the dimensions of this majestic estate. It sits on .eight parklike acres, and Lake Linton is its western border.

Several talented, farsighted couples purchased the home in July, 1985, and after months of restoration work, opened it as an inn in May, 1986. It is elegant and exceptionally comfortable, with fine furnishings

befitting the period including many large Oriental and Persian rugs. Thirteen sleeping rooms occupy the mansion and another five are located in the adjacent guesthouse.

A first-floor dining room in the mansion serves lunch and dinner Tuesday through Saturday by reservation only. Prices range from five to ten dollars for lunch entrées and fifteen to twenty-four dollars for dinner. A Continental breakfast is served to overnight guests. If you visit during the growing season, take some time to stroll through the inn's kitchen herb garden. It is the source for seasonings and garnishes used throughout the year. And ask about the special presentations given by owner Kathryn Kinney on the history and uses of herbs.

Besides being a romantic getaway, large common rooms and the availability of full food service make Montague Inn especially well suited for business meetings, receptions, and parties.

Vitals

rooms: 18, 16 with private baths

pets: no

pets in residence: none

smoking: common areas only

open season: year-round

rates: $40 through $90 single, add $5 per room double occupancy

rates include: Continental breakfast

owners: Les and Marion Tincknell, Norm and Kathryn Kinney, Aaron and Ann Acker, John and Meg Ideker, Mike and Carole Kiefer

innkeeper:
  Meg Brodie-Ideker
  1581 South Washington
  Saginaw, MI 48601
  (517) 752-3939

Murphy Inn
St. Clair

The Murphy Inn has been hosting overnight guests since 1836, and according to owner Ron Sabotka, it is the oldest commercial building in St. Clair. In fact, it occupied the site before the city of St. Clair was platted. When Ron bought it in June, 1985, he decided to retain its original name. A lot of people had been staying there for years, he explained, "And no matter what we might call it, it would always be known as the Murphy Inn!"

This place is a lot of fun. The main floor has a casual, country-theme

dining room on one side and a bar on the other, with a combined capacity of eighty people. The back bar was built in 1906 by the Brunswick Company and is set off handsomely by the room's kelly green and white print wallpaper. Much of the clientele is local, which is usually a sign of good food and personable service. We found both to be true. The staff was friendly and chatty, and the nachos and sandwiches were great, as promised. Also included on the menu were turkey and roast beef croissants, diet plates, salads, and cheesecakes. Our only regret was that we could not stay through Saturday night, when they pack the place for a sing-along.

During renovation of the inn, the original twelve small upstairs sleeping rooms were combined to make seven large rooms with private

baths. They have been extensively redecorated with beautiful print wall-paper and plush carpeting. The beds are all new and very comfortable. Nearly all the wooden turn-of-the-century dressers, vanities, and wash-stands have been in the hotel for several decades. Extra insulation went into the floors to improve soundproofing. Later in the evening, we could occasionally hear quiet laughter drifting up from the bar. It is a pleasant sound, that of friends having a good time, and we drifted effortlessly off to sleep.

Many of the inn's overnight guests come to St. Clair by boat and dock at the marina just half a block away. Guests who golf can enjoy playing at the St. Clair Golf Club, where special arrangements can be made for them through the inn. Two other courses are within fifteen miles. Those who want to take a stroll may head for the boardwalk. It is said to be the longest ever built along fresh water.

Vitals

rooms: 7 with private baths

pets: no

pets in residence: none

smoking: yes

open season: year-round

rates: $52 through $75 double occupancy

rates include: Continental breakfast

owners/innkeepers:
   Ron and Cindy Sabotka
   505 Clinton
   St. Clair, MI 48079
   (313) 329-7118

Oakbrook Inn
Davison

This magnificent pillared mansion is located back from the road in a parklike setting of rolling lawn and mature trees. Oakbrook's original two-story section and west wing were built in 1938. The east wing, with its large lounge area, was added thirty years later, and it is there that guests are most often greeted by owners Jan and Bill Cooke. They are easygoing, amiable hosts who have brought to this majestic structure the classic warmth and pace of a casual country inn.

Their lounge is furnished at one end with big, comfortable groupings of couches and chairs, a TV, and a pool table. At the other end are tables where breakfast is served and guests gather to chat over cups of coffee. Beyond the lounge is an enclosed twenty-by-forty-foot pool and an adjacent built-in bar with a refrigerator where guests may store beverages.

There are seven sleeping rooms, all spacious and very pretty. Print wallpaper set off lovely antique bedsteads and an assortment of oak washstands, vanities, dressers, and handsome glass lamps. You will also find hand-stitched quilts and pillows that were made by Jan. The three second-floor rooms are reached by a sweeping stairway that wraps around the original main entrance. Another three are just off the pool area, including the huge Master Bedroom that has a sauna and a sunken tub with a whirlpool. The entire home is plushly carpeted, tastefully decorated, and comfortable.

Jan and Bill opened Oakbrook for bed-and-breakfast lodging in spring, 1985. They are gracious innkeepers, and they spend as much time with their guests as possible. The home seems well suited for small groups and conferences. Often, says Jan, it is rented by friends who just want to get away for a few days and relax. A Continental breakfast is served each morning. Catered meals for groups can be arranged. For extended stays, you may want to inquire about the small two-bedroom cottage on the property. It is available for minimum stays of one week and has complete cooking facilities.

Vitals

rooms: 7 in the inn with private baths

pets: no

pets in residence: 1 dog and 1 cat, not allowed in guest quarters

smoking: lounge area only

open season: year-round

rates: $50 through $80 double occupancy

rates include: Continental breakfast

owners/innkeepers:

    Jan and Bill Cooke

    7256 East Court Street

    Davison, MI 48423

    (313) 658-1546

    (313) 653-1744

Raymond House Inn
Port Sanilac

Oliver Raymond was in his mid-eighties when Shirley Denison purchased his family's home from him, and he was the third generation of Raymonds to have lived there. He was a frequent visitor at the inn and provided Shirley and her guests with firsthand history of the estate. We had the privilege of meeting Mr. Raymond one evening when he came to visit. We learned that the bedroom adjacent to the dining room was for years the birthing room, and it was there, around the turn of the century, that he and several siblings were born.

Grandfather Uri Raymond came to Port Sanilac in 1850 and established a successful mercantile business. He built the handsome brick home with its distinctive white icicle trim in 1871. Shirley attributes the excellent condition of the house to the fact that it was in the same family for more than one hundred years and was never left empty or abandoned.

Shirley spent her childhood summers in Port Sanilac and had long admired the stately Raymond home. When it came up for sale, she knew she had to have it. She also knew that she would make very few changes, wanting it to closely resemble the days when three generations of Raymonds walked its wide and tall-ceilinged halls.

There are seven sleeping rooms open to guests, and they are all large, bright, and colorfully decorated. Like the parlor and dining room, they are furnished with lovely antiques, rockers, handloomed rugs, and lacy curtains as well as many old photographs. Some of the rooms have sitting areas, and there are dressers so guests can unpack for a few days. This is a good place to come with a stack of books, a list of unwritten

letters, or a folio of unfinished reports. A Continental breakfast is served each morning in the formal dining room or on an adjacent patio.

While innkeeping in this picturesque harbor town may be a relatively new career to Shirley, surrounding herself with history and art is not. For several years, she worked as a restorative artist for museums and in the United States Capitol, and she has exhibited her own sculpture and pottery in galleries in the East. Shirley's gallery and studio at the Raymond House Inn feature her wheel-thrown pottery, which is glazed and fired on the premises. If you are interested in antiques, inquire about the antique shows that Shirley hosts on the lawn of the inn during the summer and about her sister's shop just a block and a half down the street.

Vitals

rooms: 7 rooms with private baths

pets: no

pets in residence: none

smoking: parlor only

open season: May through October

rates: $45 double occupancy Sunday through Thursday, $55 Friday and Saturday

rates include: Continental breakfast

owner/innkeeper:
Shirley Denison
111 South Ridge Street (M-25)
Port Sanilac, MI 48469
(313) 622-8800

Vickie Van's Bed and Breakfast
Lexington

Vickie Van's bed-and-breakfast home is filled with personal treasures, and around most of the pieces is woven a story. "These are all the things I've grown up with," she said as she gestured around the room. She pointed to a mannequin in the corner wearing a pale pink, lace-trimmed dress, the same dress her mother is wearing in a nearby portrait painted several years ago. There are other family pictures and furnishings that have been passed on to Vickie from her parents. They are fine pieces, like the canopy and brass beds that are accented with beautiful linens and the turn-of-the-century wicker. Lace curtains in all the windows add a romantic touch.

Vickie bought the home in February, 1985, and opened the following June. One of her unexpected pleasures was getting the chance to talk with a woman who had lived in the home nearly fifty years ago. Tax records indicate that the structure was built in 1847. It sits on five

acres, and if you hit the season right, you can help Vickie pick blackberries from her bushes. When we talked to her in mid-August they were heavy with fruit. Vickie can also direct you to several pick-your-own fruit farms in the area for blueberries, raspberries, and strawberries.

Guests often gather in the game and TV room. It is informal and cozy—just a few steps down from the adjacent kitchen where Vickie is often busy preparing treats for the next morning. Breakfast varies daily, with selections that include homemade muffins, croissants, cheese and sausage, juices, and fresh fruit or fruit salad. It is served on dishes that belonged to Vickie's grandmother.

"All my dreams are coming true here," Vickie said unabashedly. She thoroughly enjoys running a bed-and-breakfast home and cares deeply for her guests. "Every person is a story," she recounted. "People open

up to me and they talk a lot here. I try to make each person's day a little bit better."

Vitals

rooms: 4, 2 with private baths and 2 that share 1 bath

pets: no

pets in residence: 1 cat and 1 dog, not allowed in guest rooms or dining area

smoking: not in the house

open season: year-round

rates: $45 shared bath, $50 private bath, 10 percent discount Sunday through Thursday

rates include: breakfast

owner/innkeeper:
Vickie Van
5076 South Lakeshore Road
Lexington, MI 48450
(313) 359-5533

The Victorian Inn
Port Huron

This fine Queen Anne structure was designed by architect Isaac Erb and built as a residence for James A. Davidson and his family in 1896. Davidson grew up in Port Huron and established a huge home furnishings company there that occupied three adjacent storefronts on Military Street.

Ed and Vicki Peterson and Lew and Lynne Secory became the home's fourth set of owners when they purchased it in 1983. They were pleased to find that the original plans and specification sheets passed on to them were still in good order, providing great assistance in the renovation. Three months after their purchase, the home was judged historically and architecturally significant by the Michigan Historical Commission and was listed on the State Register of Historic Places.

The four second-floor sleeping rooms are furnished with period pieces, particularly Queen Anne, and dressed with yards of lace and finery. Warm tones of peach and rose are used for most of the walls,

linens, and floor coverings. They provide a backdrop for Victorian-era memorabilia such as a collection of hatboxes, a nosegay, a wicker bed tray, and a beribboned wreath of baby's breath and dried flowers. The effect is romantic and very pretty.

The inn's elegant first-floor dining room is open to the public, with lunch and dinner offerings such as beef rosettes with duxelles, veal chops with morel sauce, the chef's special cream of peanut soup, and homemade ice cream. The floor staff is formally attired—an appropriate touch in this genteel setting. The cellar has been converted to Pierpont's Pub, where stone walls and an embossed tin ceiling lend a more casual atmosphere. It features live music on Thursday and Friday nights.

A Continental breakfast of freshly baked croissants, coffee, and juice is served each morning to overnight guests.

Vitals

rooms: 4, 2 with private baths

pets: no

pets in residence: none

smoking: yes, but discouraged in sleeping rooms

open season: year-round

rates: $45 through $65 per double room

rates include: Continental breakfast

owners/innkeepers:

Ed and Vicki Peterson
Lew and Lynne Secory
1229 7th Street
Port Huron, MI 48060
(313) 984-1437

Wood's Inn
Ann Arbor

Barbara Inwood's home is nestled in a fine old, wooded neighborhood just a half block off the picturesque Huron River. Its ivy-covered exterior and beautiful gardens are reminiscent of the cottages of rural England.

The original section of the home is solid stone construction that dates to 1859. Inside, you can see the deep windowsills that are formed by the thickness of the sturdy walls. The newer clapboard addition was added before 1900. Early American and primitive antiques give a snug, comfortable feeling and a strong sense of history.

"I collect everything," Barbara confessed. And while that may be a bit of an exaggeration, we discovered she has a special fondness for trinket boxes and Currier and Ives prints. A big map on the wall in the sitting room is stuck with pins that document Barbara's world travels. You will notice a profusion of pins fanning out from London where she taught school for a year and discovered the joys of bed-and-breakfast travel during her spare time. Her excursions into the English, Scottish, and Welsh countrysides convinced Barbara to try her own hand at innkeeping.

There are four sleeping rooms for guests, and each of the beds is covered with an antique quilt. Guests who prefer first-floor accommodations will enjoy Jeffrey's Room, located just off the sitting room. It is furnished with a cannonball double bed and a lovely appliqued quilt that was made by the family's Great Aunt Mary. When all the sleeping rooms are occupied, Barbara takes up residence in the hired-hand's room off the kitchen.

Guests are treated to a full, sit-down breakfast that includes fruits, breads, casseroles, and other specialties. "I pay attention to cholesterol, whole grains, and other food considerations, because I know most of my guests are diet conscious," Barbara explained. They enjoy the repast in the big, wicker-furnished winterized porch that Barbara says is a favorite spot for guests to gather year-round.

It is quiet and peaceful here, yet only five minutes from downtown Ann Arbor and the University of Michigan campus. Newly retired from her position as a principal, Barbara divides her time between gardening, raising champion dalmatians, planning new travels, enjoying her family, and caring for her guests. She has a delightfully adventurous spirit and a gift for good conversation.

Vitals

rooms: 4; 2 with private baths, 2 that share 1 bath

pets: by special arrangement

pets in residence: 2 dogs and 1 cat, not permitted in guest rooms

smoking: in designated areas

open season: year-round

rates: $45 through $50 single or double occupancy

rates include: breakfast

owner/innkeeper:
Barbara Inwood
2887 Newport Road
Ann Arbor, MI 48103
(313) 665-8394

Bed-and-Breakfast
Reservation Services

The following descriptions are of bed-and-breakfast reservation services. Although we have not used any of the services and have not visited all the homes they represent, we offer them to you as another means of locating bed-and-breakfast lodging at your destination point.

Bed and Breakfast of Grand Rapids
Grand Rapids

The Heritage Hill district of Grand Rapids boasts representation of more than sixty architectural styles—the largest collection of any historic district in the country. The homes were built between 1850 and 1920, and they cover several blocks on the eastern perimeter of the downtown.

Bed and Breakfast of Grand Rapids is a reservation service that places overnight guests in private homes within the historic district. A variety of accommodations is available. Proprietor Dorothy Stout helps match the special needs and interests of guests with the offerings of host families.

This is an excellent opportunity to learn about the district and to spend some time in marvelous historic homes that you might otherwise only see from the sidewalk.

Bed and Breakfast of Grand Rapids
Dorothy Stout
455 College S.E.
Grand Rapids, MI 49503
(616) 451-4849 or (616) 459-9055

Bed and Breakfast in Michigan

Diane Shields is the new owner of this reservation service and has listings throughout the Lower Peninsula of Michigan. Most accommodations are in private homes or small guesthouses located in the Detroit area as well as Ann Arbor, the thumb region, along the Lake Michigan shoreline, and northern resort areas. To secure reservations, send Diane a self-addressed stamped envelope and request a directory of her participating homes. She updates it frequently. Each listing includes a brief description of the home or guesthouse and its general location. You can also call Diane after 6:00 p.m. and on weekends. Room rates range from forty through seventy-five dollars double occupancy, with a single about five dollars less.

Bed and Breakfast in Michigan
Diane Shields
P.O. Box 1731
Dearborn, MI 48121-1731
(313) 561-6041

Frankenmuth Area Bed and Breakfast Reservation Service
Frankenmuth

If you plan to partake in the Bavarian-style festivities of the town of Frankenmuth, you can reserve bed-and-breakfast accommodations through this local reservation service. Host homes offer from two to four sleeping rooms. Reservations are made through a central number and payment is made directly to the reservation service rather than the host. Coordinator Beverley Bender says that promotes the feeling of being a guest in the home. Early reservations are helpful, but drop-ins are welcome. Rates range from forty through sixty dollars double occupancy with a Continental breakfast.

Frankenmuth Area Bed and Breakfast Reservation Service
337 Trinklein Street
Frankenmuth, MI 48734
Beverley Bender
(517) 652-8897

Index